Generis
PUBLISHING

THE PHILOSOPHY OF EXTERNAL PUBLIC DEBT MANAGEMENT

ANI ZOHRAB GRIGORYAN

Title: **THE PHILOSOPHY OF EXTERNAL PUBLIC DEBT MANAGEMENT**

ISBN: 979-8-89248-836-5

Author: ANI ZOHRAB GRIGORYAN

Cover image: https://pixabay.com/illustrations/businesswoman-business-career-6557677/

Publisher: Generis Publishing
Online orders: www.generis-publishing.com
Contact email: info@generis-publishing.com

THE PHILOSOPHY OF EXTERNAL PUBLIC DEBT MANAGEMENT

ANI ZOHRAB GRIGORYAN

Contents

INTRODUCTION

Effective management of external public debt acquires key importance especially in crisis situations. The 2008 financial crisis, which began with the US mortgage market, was the second deepest after the Great Depression of the 1930s. As a result of the crisis, negative consequences were manifested in all countries. The financial and economic crisis was followed by the Covid-19 pandemic.

The purpose of the book is to analyze and evaluate the effectiveness of external public debt management and propose ways to improve management in accordance with the time. In connection with the purpose of the book, the following tasks were proposed:

- to study public debt management strategy, identifying tangible risks,

- to develop an approach of factor analysis in terms of justifying the reduction of the share of external public debt and the increase of internal borrowed funds in the structure of public debt,

- to substantiate and propose the expediency of applying the most appropriate approaches developed by the largest international research structures in the concept of assessing the burden of the national debt,

- to estimate the ratio of real salary, average monthly salary and indicators of government bonds using the correlation method,

- to estimate the ratio of the average monthly salary and external public debt using the correlation and regression methods,

- to carry out multiple linear regression and correlation assessment between indicators of economic activity, exchange rate (AMD/The average exchange rate of 1 US dollar) and the external public debt, having checked the results using the Shapiro–Wilk test.

CHAPTER 1. THEORETICAL, METHODOLOGICAL AND LEGISLATIVE BASES OF FOREIGN STATE DEBT MANAGEMENT

1.1 Philosophical perceptions of the debt problem and the history of defaults of European Countries until the 20th century

External debt is one of the most common sources of financing budget deficits, which are currently very diverse. At the current stage of economic development, almost all countries are not immune to external public debt. For developed countries, external debt is not a cause for concern, as long as they are solvent, but in the case of developing countries, the constant growth of external debt is problematic.

In spite of the different philosophical accounts of debt, a constant element runs throughout the debt literature as an uninterrupted thread, namely that debt repayment is conceived as a fundamental obligation, one that the debtor cannot and should not circumvent without costs. Indeed, the act of non-repayment does not only mark the transgression of a contract, which is punishable by law, but also and foremost the betrayal of a promise, which is something morally wrong.[1] In this reading, the inability of giving back what is owed necessarily entails a slip down the moral ladder.[2]

Debt has become a paramount topic of discussion and controversy in recent times, fuelled by the financial crisis of 2008 and the different episodes of the sovereign debt crisis in Europe, above all involving Greece. This has produced a great deal of commentaries, economic analyses, and journalistic polemics from all sides of the political spectrum. Yet despite this profusion of discourse, it still proves difficult to seize the exact contours of the problem. Debt affects both the most isolated individuals and the most powerful states, it is equally a matter of "cold" economic rationality and the "hottest" emotions and moral judgments, it

[1] Kant, I., (2002). "Groundwork for the Metaphysics of Morals", trans. A. W. Wood, Yale University Press, New Haven, p. 39

[2] Stefanutti, S. (2020). "Philosophy of Debt: In Search of the Relationship Between Debts and Duties", No (2020)
https://doi.org/10.7413/24208914074

appears at once as the most empirical thing with the hardest material consequences and as a mysterious, ethereal, abstract, and purely speculative entity (the unreal product of financial "speculation"). The concept of indebtedness not only characterizes an increasingly universal economic predicament, but also defines a form of subjectivity central to our present condition.[3]

In this context, studying the debt problem, we discuss various aspects on which various approaches of well-known theorists have been formed.

Alexander Douglas careful reflections – historical, semantic, logical and practical – suggest that the 'obvious' point of view is at best misleading and at worse pernicious, especially in a global economic system that is in its essence dependent on government-managed debt.

Douglas looks at debt in the ancient world, with its pattern of high interest loans to subsistence farmers in times of crisis (war, drought etc.), leading to loss of possessions (and thus earning-potential) and the sale of family members into various forms of slavery. He also notes the need for periodic amnesties (like the Biblical Jubilee) where debts were cancelled and slaves returned to their families, not simply as a matter of justice, but in order to prevent revolution. Out of this experience – the exploitation of the poor in forcing them to borrow to survive a crisis beyond their control (forced debt) – springs the ancient condemnation of usury, from the criticisms of Aristotle to the censures of medieval church councils. Here there is very limited evidence for the common utility of the institution of debt, and thus limited grounds for any absolute moral obligation to pay in full all interest-based loans.

Sometimes usury does allow for idle savings to be put to good uses. But sometimes it allows them to be put to *bad* uses. Chief among the latter is the activity of rich usurers, with savings to spare, lending to the very poor at rates that ultimately ensure that they will end up even poorer. The very poor will nevertheless take the loans on these terms out of desperation.

Thus debt as an institution is morally ambivalent. Clearly there is a good, mutually beneficial set of debt-related practices. But we cannot insist on an

---

[3] Santner E. & Schuster A. (2016-2017 Autumn). "The debt drive: Philosophy, psychoanalysis, neoliberalism", Retrieved October 3, 2022, available at the following link: https://english.uchicago.edu/courses/debt-drive-philosophy-psychoanalysis-neoliberalism

absolute obligation to pay debts, without considering the quality and effects of all debt-related activity in society at large.

Douglas goes on to an apparent digression on money. In fact, this discussion establishes the unique role of sovereign government in the social web of debt, production and social security, which derives from the nature of money.

In 1931 it came as a surprise to the British government to discover that it could come off the gold standard without the pound collapsing. But, says Douglas, 'Only when the gold promise ceased to be honored did the explanation become clear: the paper notes themselves were acceptable for tax payments, and this gave them a value of their own, independent of their redeemability for anything else.' This has radical consequences for the way we think about government debt.[4]

As is the case with all economic concepts, and when setting goals in the process of public debt management, there is still no consensus among economists. However, according to one of the most common points of view, the main goal of public debt management is to minimize the cost of servicing it and, as a result, the state receives loans on the most favorable terms. In this case, the mechanism of public debt management is quite simple, since the state at the stage of economic recovery tries not to take long-term loans whenever possible, so that in the future you do not have to pay for them amounts with high nominal interest rates. Therefore, in order to avoid this during an economic downturn, the government of this country takes the opposite actions, that is, sets a goal to attract new loans by increasing the terms of debt obligations, mainly in the form of long-term loans.[5]

Local and foreign literature, scientific publications of well-known researchers interested in the problem were the research basis for the researchers.

The authors used the scientific analytical method as a research method, emphasizing the tools of generalized philosophical conclusions.

"Philosophy of Economics" consists of inquiries concerning

(a) rational choice,

---

[4] Douglas, A., X. (2016a.). "The philosophy of debt", *Routledge. Retrieved October 3, 2022, available at the following link:* https://www.thinkingfaith.org/-articles/philosophy-debt

[5] Rusyaykina, A. M. (2001). Penza, "Public debt management", p.11.

(b) the evaluation of economic outcomes, institutions and processes, and

(c) the ontology of economic phenomena and the possibilities of acquiring knowledge of them.

Although these inquiries overlap in many ways, it is useful to divide philosophy of economics in this way into three subject matters which can be regarded respectively as branches of action theory, ethics (or normative social and political philosophy), and philosophy of science. Economic theories of rationality, welfare, and social choice defend substantive philosophical theses often informed by relevant philosophical literature and of evident interest to those interested in action theory, philosophical psychology, and social and political philosophy. Economics is of particular interest to those interested in epistemology and philosophy of science both because of its detailed peculiarities and because it possesses many of the overt features of the natural sciences, while its object consists of social phenomena.[6]

In practice, the amount of debt may increase or be subject to adjustments if the financial system continues to operate as a result. For debt in circulation to keep increasing, the amount of demands for loans must keep increasing. This, in turn, presupposes an unsustainable and environmentally damaging rate of economic growth. At the same time, if the government wants money it too must borrow, so that a portion of taxes are used to pay interest owed to the banks. Many do continue to wonder why the government does not change the system and find a way of creating money itself. The answer usually offered (amongst the few that consider these matters) is the temptation would be there for those in power to use the money to meet their debts and pledges and buy votes, etc., with the result that hard-won trust in money would soon dissipate.[7]

---

[6] Philosophy of Economics (2003/2018). In Stanford Encyclopedia of Philosophy. Retrieved October 3, 2022 available at the following link: https://plato.stanford.edu/entries/economics/

[7] Lawson, T. (2016). "The philosophy of debt'. The Philosophers Magazine: 10.5840/tpm20167223, available at the following link:
https://www.researchgate.net/publication/296687370_The_philosophy_of_debt p.17

It is also worth noting that when debt reaches a certain level, foreign investors and creditors become more cautious about investments, which undermines economic growth.[8]

Finance and philosophy may seem to be worlds apart. But they share at least one common ancestor: Thales of Miletus. Thales is typically regarded as the first philosopher, but he was also a financial innovator. He appears to have been what we would now call an option trader. He predicted that next year's olive harvest would be good, and therefore paid a small amount of money to the owners of olive presses for the right to the next year's use. When the harvest turned out to be as good as predicted, Thales earned a sizable amount of money by renting out the presses.[9]

Coins have largely been replaced by either paper or electronic money, and we have built a large infrastructure to facilitate transactions of money and other financial assets - with elements including commercial banks, central banks, insurance companies, stock exchanges, and investment funds. This institutional multiplicity is due to concerted efforts of both private and public agents, as well as innovations in financial economics and in the financial industry.[10]

Our ethical and political sensitivities have also changed in several respects. It seems fair to say that most traditional ethicists held a very negative attitude towards financial activities. Think, for example, of Jesus' cleansing of the temple from moneylenders, and the widespread condemnation of money as "the root of all evil". Attitudes in this regard seem to have softened over time. However, the moral debate continues to recur, especially in connection with large scandals and crises within finance, the largest such crisis in recent memory of course being the global financial crisis of 2008.[11]

---

[8] Makaryan, A., Hayrapetian A. (2021). "State debt threshold indicators". International research and armenian reality, Proceedings of the Armenian State University of Economics, 4/2021, available at the following link:
https://arar.sci.am/dlibra/publication/321590/edition/294748/content

[9] Aristotle (1984) Politics J. Barnes, The Complete Works of Aristotle: Book 1, section1252a: Princeton University Press, available at the following link:
http://www.perseus.tufts.edu/hopper/text?doc=urn:cts:greekLit:tlg0086.tlg035.perseus-eng1

[10] Shiller, R. J., (2012). "*Finance and the Good Society*", Princeton: Princeton University Press.

[11] Philosophy of Money and Finance (2018). In Stanford Encyclopedia of Philosophy. Retrieved October 3, 2022 available at the following link:
https://plato.stanford.edu/entries/money-finance/

In particular, the COVID-19 pandemic, which followed the financial crisis, created new challenges in the global economic system, further aggravating the costs of countries, measures to overcome which are still being implemented.

Take the first question: why should I pay my debts? It's easy to be tempted by simple answers, such as 'because I said I would', 'because I owe it to my creditor' or 'because it's just the right thing to do'. Yet although these answers make legal sense, they don't quite work philosophically-speaking. They all sound like universal principles, but the obligation to repay debts is a very particular thing, depending on the particulars of the case.

Debt and duty – despite having roots in the same word (the Latin, *debitum*) – are not always the same thing. Paying debts is of course the right thing to do, but not always. What we need is an explanation of why it is usually the right thing to do – universal principles won't do the trick.[12]

The State has the task of determining the juridical framework within which economic affairs are to be conducted, and thus of safeguarding the prerequisites of a free economy, which presumes a certain equality between the parties, such that one party would not be so powerful as to reduce the other to subservience.

Economics understood in abstraction ... is not just an academic error: it actually dismantles the walls of the home. Appealing to the market as an independent authority ... has meant in many contexts over the last few decades a ruinous legacy for heavily indebted countries, large-scale and costly social disruption even in developed economies; and, most recently, the extraordinary phenomena of a financial trading world in which the marketing of toxic debt became the driver of money-making – until the bluffs were all called at the same time.

There have been many remarkable anthropological and sociological studies of debt and related institutions. Philosophy can contribute to the ensuing

[12] Douglas, A. X. (2020). "What do I owe? The philosophy of debt". Article updated on: 20 January available at the following link: https://www.iwoca.co.uk/insights/philosophy-of-debt-part-one/

discussion and help us to keep our language precise and discover the implicit principles contained in our intuitions.[13]

According to B. A. Heifetz[14] (n.d.) public debt is broadly characterized as outstanding financial obligations of the state and its authorized body in relation to residents and non-residents M. Fedosov, S. Ya. Sutormina, V. M. Ogorodnik believe that "public debt is the amount of outstanding debt obligations on domestic government loans, as well as the amount of financial obligations of the country to foreign creditors at a certain point in time."[15] According to K. McConnell[16] (1992) "the public debt is the size of the positive balance of the state budget and the deficit". A. Dolan and K. Campbell believe that the public debt is the accumulated amount of budget deficits over previous years.[17]

In the explanatory economic dictionary, public debt is interpreted as the total amount of debt owed by the government of a country to the owners of securities, equal to the amount of the budget deficit in the past, minus the budget surplus.[18] Another approach defines that the public debt is the size of the state's internal and external obligations to its creditors.[19]

The above definitions are summarized in the Law of the Republic of Armenia "On public debt", according to which the state debt is the sum of the

---

[13] Douglas, (2015). "The Philosophy of Debt". 23 November, available at the following link: https://www.taylorfrancis.com/books/mono/10.4324/9781315681009/philosophy-debt-alexander-douglas

[14] Heifetz, B. A. (2022). "Gosudarstvennyi dolg (Public debt in Russian), In Bol'shaya rossiiskaya entsiklopediya
(Great Russian Encyclopedia, in Russian) available at the following link: https://bigenc.ru/economis/text/2373368

[15] Fedoov, V.M., Buryak L.D., Butakov D.D. (1991) ed. Fedosova V. M., Ogorodnik S.Y a and Sutormina V. N. – K Lybid, Public finance Proc. A manual for students of economic universities and faculty / 1991.–276 p. ISBN 5-11-001607-0. available at the following link: https://kneu.edu.ua/ua/science_kneu/%20scientific_schools/spf/spf_praci/spf_prazi/gosfin/

[16] McConnell, K. R. (1992). "Economics: Principles, probl. and Politics": In 2 vols. Vol. 1 / K. R. McConnell, S. L. Brue. M.: Respublika, p. 365

[17] Dolan, E. J., Money, banking and monetary policy / E. J. Dolan, C. D. Campbell, R. J. Campbell, trans. from English V. V. Lukashevich and others. St. Petersburg: St. Petersburg Orchestra, 1994. p. 402

[18] Kirakosyan, G. E., Ghushchyan H. B., Tigranyan I. T. (1999). "Economic Explanatory Dictionary", Yerevan, Economist, pp. 342-343.

[19] Avetisyan, I. A. (2001). Fundamentals of financial management at the macro level (questions of theory and methodology). Vologda, p. 194

debt of the Government and the debt of the Central Bank. The components of public debt are domestic public debt, external public debt and government guarantees.[20]

In principle, we can agree with the above definitions of public debt, which have almost the same meaning. At the same time, they emphasize two circumstances: the mechanism of the formation of public debt and the formulation of public debt. It can be concluded that the definitions presented in the professional literature, together with their philosophical concepts, are not sufficiently holistic and can be supplemented taking into account the peculiarities of the formation of public debt and how diversified its impact on the economy are. We believe that public debt is the result of financial relations, when temporarily available funds as a result of borrowing from the private sector or from abroad are transferred to the state budget.[21]

The past half century has witnessed the emergence of a large literature on economic methodology, presenting many methodological approaches and conclusions that apply to many schools and branches of economics. Much of the literature has focused primarily on the fundamental theory of economics, namely the theory of equilibrium resulting from bounded rational individual choice, but macroeconomics is of enormous importance in determining the appropriate responses to the recession since 2008 in the daily work of economists, coupled with the rapidly increasing role of empirical and experimental research, finding responses in methodological inquiries.[22]

Reinhart, Rogoff and Savastano[23] studied the cycles of capital flows to developing countries over the past two hundred years and came to the conclusion that debtors and creditors change, however, the nature of the cycles has remained

---

[20] RA Law "On State Debt", 2008 article 5, article 6, available at the following link: https://www.arlis.am/documentview.aspx?docid=119085

[21] Vardanyan, K., Avagyan G. & Karapetyan N. (2021). "INTERPRETATION OF THE THEORIES AND THE RESULTS OF EMPIRICAL RESEARCH ON PUBLIC DEBT MANAGEMENT AND THE IMPACT OF DEBT ON ECONOMIC GROWTH". PUBLIC ADMINISTRATION 1/2021, available at the following link: https://paara.am/wp-content/uploads/2012/06/qnarik-vardanyan-gayane-avagyan.pdf

[22] Backhouse, R. & Fontaine P._(Eds., (2010). "The Unsocial Social Science? Economics and Neighboring Disciplines since 1945", Durham, NC: Duke University Press

[23] Reinhart, C. M., Rogoff. K. S., Savastano, M. A. (2003). DEBT INTOLERANCE.NATIONAL BUREAU OF ECONOMIC RESEARCH. Working Paper 9908. http://www.nber.org/papers/w9908

the same over time. When interest rates and stock profitability are low and liquidity is high, investors look elsewhere for high profitability. At such times, it is easy for developing country governments to raise funds from external sources, which they do. But history has shown that for many countries, raising debt leads to insolvency.

A history of multiple defaults suggests that large capital inflows to such countries end in insolvency. According to these authors, the acceptable upper limit of public debt is specific for each country and depends on the history of previous defaults and the history of inflation.

Table 1.

The History of Defaults of European Countries until the 20th Century[24]

(Kyurumyan A. 2014 p. 53)

		1501-1800 years of defaults		1801-1900 years of defaults	Total
	Quantity		Quantity		
Spain	6	1557,1575,1607,1627,1647	7	1820,1831,1834,1851,1867,1872,1882	13
France	8	1558,1624,1648,1661,1701,1715,1770,1788	-	-	8
Portugal	1	1560	5	1837,1841,1845,1852,1890	6
Germany	1	1683	5	1807,1812,1813,1814,1850	6
Austria	-	-	5	1802,1805,18611,1816,1868	5
Greece	-	-	4	1826,1843,1860,1893	4
Bulgaria	-	-	2	1886,1891	2
Poland	-	-	1	1814	1
Russia	-	-	1	1839	1
Total	16		30		46

[24] Kyurumyan, A. (2014). “Thepolicy decisions and consequenceson public debt management in recent years”, p. 53, available at the following link: https://www.osf.am/wp-content/uploads/2014/04/Debt-Managment_Artak-Kyurumyan.pdf

Public debts are high and rising. And the world worries. Academic economists worry that the "long-term trend in debt accumulation seems inconsistent with theories of optimal government debt policies."[25] Portfolio managers and financial regulators worry about the shrinking universe of safe assets, excessive risk-taking, and the corresponding threats to financial stability. International financial institutions worry that if history is any guide, (e.g. Sandleris, 2016)[26] current debt levels likely carry the seeds of future trouble involving some painful combination of sovereign default, high inflation, and financial collapse.

In the case of some debt-intolerant countries, its maximum permissible volume does not exceed 15 percent of GDP. According to Reinhart, Rogoff and Savastano[27], knowing the level of debt intolerance is important for making decisions on the stability and restructuring of debt, the integration of capital markets and the volumes of funds raised from external sources to mitigate the effects of the crisis.

Eden, Kraay and Qian[28] (2012) studied 118 cases of default and 282 cases of foreign investment expropriation by 172 countries in 1970-2004 and concluded that although defaults and expropriations occur in the same countries in the long run, they do not in the short run. In only five cases, these events occurred in the same year. Defaults are more likely to occur after periods of rapid debt accumulation when economic growth is low.

Bi, Shen and Yang[29] (2014) examined the effects of fiscal consolidation and government spending under different levels of debt burden and found that fiscal consolidation has a negative effect on GDP. In cases of high debt burdens, increased government spending pushes the economy closer to fiscal policy limits, increasing risk and the associated premium that investors overlook, as well as the likelihood of default. With high debt burdens, the expansionary effect of

---

[25] Yared, P (2019), "Rising Government Debt: Causes and Solutions for a Decades-Old Trend," *Journal of Economic Perspectives* 33(2): pp. 115-140.

[26] Sandleris, G. (2016), "The Costs of Sovereign Defaults: Theory and Empirical Evidence," *Economia* 16(2): 1-27

[27] Reinhart, Rogoff, Savastano (2003), Bosher (1970), Vives (1969), Winkler (1933) and Wynne (1951)

[28] Eden, Maya, Kraay Aart & Qian Rong. (2012). Sovereign Defaults and Expropriations Empirical Regularities. The World Bank Policy Research Working Paper 6218.

[29] Bi, Huixin, Shen, Wenyi and Yang, Shu-Chun. (2014). "Fiscal Limits, External Debt, and Fiscal Policy in Developing Countries". IMF Working Paper #49. March 2014

government spending growth is smaller than with low debt burdens and may increase the probability of default.

According to Stiglitz, the costs associated with servicing the public debt of a number of developing countries exceeded twenty-five percent of exports[30] (Stiglitz, 2002) and even fifty (Stiglitz, 2007). Stiglitz also refers to the so-called "odious" debt provided for political purposes during the Cold War, and expresses the opinion that nations should not pay for these loans instead of the enriched ruling administration, and creditors themselves should take into account the possibility of losing their money in such cases[31]. Today, the citizens of Chile continue to pay the debts taken by the Pinochet government, the citizens of the South African Republic continue to pay the apartheid debts, until recently, Argentina was still paying off debts incurred to finance a "dirty war" waged against its own people by the junta that seized power in 1976-83, during which nearly 30,000 Argentinians went missing. The legislative acts of Lebanon and Tunisia determine the maximum relative amount of public debt (as a percentage of GDP), and the legislation of Zambia sets the maximum absolute amount of debt.[32] In a number of countries, such as Bulgaria, Colombia, Costa Rica, Croatia, Indonesia, Lebanon, Sri Lanka and Tunisia, the maximum limit on the amount of debt that can be raised is set in the state budget laws. The laws of Bulgaria, Colombia, Croatia, Pakistan and Tunisia limit the maximum annual amounts of guarantees provided by the state.[33]

For example, studying the current debt problem of China, we consider it important to note that the debt of local governments is subjected to a special analysis.

The current local government debt problem in China has a long history, there are many problems, and the potential risks are enormous. Therefore, the Chinese central government and its subordinate governments are required to grasp the essence of local government debt problems, and based on their own functions, adopt effective measures to gradually resolve the debt problem and further reduce the local government debt risk. The reasons for the local government debt in

[30] Stiglitz, J. E. (2002). Globalization and its Discontent. W. W. Norton and company

[31] Stiglitz, J. E. (2007). Making the Globalization Work. W. W. Norton and company.

[32] World Bank. (2007). Managing Public Debt: from Diagnostics to Reform Implementation

[33] Kyurumyan, A. (2014). "Thepolicy decisions and consequenceson public debt management in recent years", p. 53 available at the following link: https://www.osf.am/wp-content/uploads/2014/04/Debt-Managment_Artak-Kyurumyan.pdf

China, such as the mismatch between the local government's power and financial resources, the concept of political achievements, and the rule of law and the rule of law reform of the financial market mechanism all take time. It needs to take into account the applicability of the current Chinese fiscal system; it is necessary to carry out a slow experimental trial and error to get a better solution, and the current economic situation of each province adopts a soft landing method to gradually carry out governance.

In the international community, the financial risk management mechanism generally adopts a quantitative management model. Then, on basis of quantification, according to the overall economic development of the country, a "linear indicator system" is established, and a "warning signal" with visual significance is also used. "Lights to monitor the current debt size". When a debt problem arises, effective measures can be taken to monitor the debt at the first time. However, China's current debt situation is relatively complicated, and there are many kinds of debts, and most of them are still in the form of implicit debt. Even if they have corresponding management measures and systems, they are subject to various objective conditions for local governments. The constraints cannot be perfected like the international community, in order to monitor and warn government debts.[34]

According to a report from the Jubilee Debt Campaign, there are currently 24 countries facing a full-blown debt crisis, with 14 more on the verge. Globally, there is about $200 trillion of debt on the books.[35]

Although the poor and disenfranchised of the world play no role in negotiating these loans, in debt crises they usually end up paying the price. So when a country borrows money, who or what is the "economic agent" responsible for taking on the debt? Can traditional economic theory explain why we face debt crises and how we can get out of them? Or do we need a new

[34] Zou, F. (2019). "Analysis and Research on Local Government Debt Problems in China". Modern Economy, 10, 188-197
https://doi.org/10.4236/me.2019.101013
https://www.scirp.org/pdf/ME_2019011716224598.pdf

[35] Kalantari, Sh. & Sholes I. (2019). available at the following link: https://www.philosophytalk.org/shows/ethics-debt

economic model that dispels some of the myths of the traditional model and offers a more ethical solution to the global debt crisis?[36]

The goal of minimizing the cost of servicing the public debt J. Tobin complements the issue of currency stabilization (dram, currency), believing that only such debt management can be beneficial for the state. At the same time, J. Tobin[37] supports this point of view also because, in his opinion, it is impossible to clearly distinguish between the spheres of public debt management and monetary policy, as well as the activity spheres of the Central Bank and the Treasury.

The definition of the goal of public debt management by Keynesians has received various interpretations. According to these theorists, the public debt was considered as a factor in achieving and maintaining economic stability, therefore, in this case, the public debt management policy is aimed at improving the efficiency of the economic incentive system.[38] In this case, the costs associated with interest payments on the public debt are minimized until, so far, it contributes to the stabilization of the economy. That is, the state at the stage of economic recovery should mainly issue long-term obligations, which, in turn, is due to an increase in the interest rate and investment demand. But during an economic downturn, based on judgments about the stabilization of the economy, it is necessary to issue short-term loans to compensate for excess liquidity.[39]

1.2 The Philosophy of Public Debt Management in Recent Years. Cases from RA

As known, the main blow of the global financial and economic crisis occurred in 2009, which began with the US mortgage market, and then spread to the whole world. By some estimates, the crisis was the deepest since the Great

---

[36] See the same https://www.philosophytalk.org/shows/ethics-debt

[37] Tobin, J. (1963). "An Essay on Principles of Debt Management". N.Y., Cowles Foundation for Research in Economics at Yale University, p. 210.

[38] Hansen, E. (1997). "Economic cycles and national income. Keynesian Classics" (vol. 2). - M.: p.334

[39] Bayadyan, A. & Markosyan, H. (2014). "The goals of public debt management and the issues of its regulation". NAS of RA, Current issues of socio-economic development in the Republic of Armenia #1/2014, 45-49 1829-4324. available at the following link: https://arar.sci.am/dlibra/publication/280667/edition/257694/content

Depression of the 1930s. The crisis affected all countries, including the Republic of Armenia. Neither the country's government nor the private sectors were prepared for this unprecedented crisis. In such circumstances, sound debt management plays an important role in process of public sector financial management. This obtains more importance for countries with small and open economies, when the domestic economy has limited resources, and the government is forced to raise debt to implement a fiscal policy conducive to economic growth.

Therefore, in such a situation, the government should be sure that the borrowing policy in the future will not lead to an unstable situation, will not increase financing costs to an unacceptable and extreme level, or will not make the country vulnerable to the development of the external world. This requires the implementation of an effective debt management system, which under favorable conditions can reduce negative impacts and mitigate potential risks.[40]

It is worth noting that during the last financial and economic crisis, almost all especially developed countries had to conduct an unprecedented stimulating economic policy in order to revive their economies... As a result, for example, in the USA and many countries of the European Union, the public debt crossed the threshold of 100% of GDP, and the monetary policy interest rate reached the zero lower limit.[41]

The economic and political reasons for increasing government debt are well understood and instruments have been deployed at both the national and the EU level, to stop and possibly revert the upward trend. However, results have been mixed at best. There are countries who have followed and will continue to follow a prudent course of action and thus manage to keep government debt comparatively low or broadly stable. At the same time, there are quite a few countries who, for a number of reasons, did not manage to keep government debt from growing relative to GDP.

---

[40] Chinaryan, V. (2012). "State debt and its management issues". National Academy of Sciences of the Republic of Armenia Current issues of socio-economic development in the Republic of Armenia #2/2012 pp. 106-109, available at the following link:
https://arar.sci.am/dlibra/publication/280508/edition/257543/content

[41] The European Central Bank reduced the asset purchase program from September 2018 and stopped it completely at the end of the year.

The economic and political reasons for increasing government debt are well understood and instruments have been deployed at both the national and the EU level, to stop and possibly revert the upward trend. However, results have been mixed at best. There are countries who have 26 followed and will continue to follow a prudent course of action and thus manage(d) to keep government debt comparatively low or broadly stable. At the same time, there are quite a few countries who, for a number of reasons, did not manage to keep government debt from growing relative to GDP.[42]

With the aim of an adequate response of the RA to economic developments in 2020 and in the medium term, the following priorities were set for fiscal policy.[43]

1. Anti- circuit policy. In accordance with the system of fiscal rules in 2020 fiscal policy will be an incentive to counteract the economic shock caused by the outbreak of the COVID-19 pandemic and the imposed economic restrictions. And starting from 2021, fiscal policy will have a neutral orientation.

2. Stimulating long-term economic growth. Fiscal policy in 2020 will deviate from the "golden rule" of state finances, which requires that the volume of government borrowings in a given year should not exceed the volume of state investments, and current expenses should be covered by own revenues. From 2021, fiscal policy will return to the "Golden Rule". Under the "Golden Rule", increasing the role of capital expenditures directed to state infrastructures will allow to promote long-term economic growth and ensure the stability of the state debt in the long run due to GDP growth.

3. Maintaining financial and debt stability. The reduction of tax revenues of the state budget in the context of the COVID-19 pandemic and the growth of current expenditures and lending to the economy due to anti-crisis actions will lead to a significant deviation of the debt burden of the RA Government from the threshold of 50% in the GDP. In the medium term, the objective of fiscal

---

[42] Larch, M. (2022). "The (un) sustainability of public debt: the elusive reality of an intuitive concept". Head of Secretariat, European Fiscal Board, 5 April 2022 pp. 25-26, available at the following link:
https://www.coleurope.eu/sites/default/files/research-paper/BEERpaper_41%20Larch%205%20April.pdf

[43] RA Ministry of Finance and Statistical Committee

policy is to smoothly reduce the debt burden to 54.7%, and then to ensure the government debt burden reduction target of 50% of GDP in the following years.

The main goal of this chapter is to propose effective solutions in the philosophical context of the management of the foreign public debt of RA. The Government of the RA should adopt as a priority the philosophy of attracting borrowed funds from the domestic market.

Considering also the fact that the Republic of Armenia relied on the philosophy of ensuring double-digit economic growth, having a long-term goal to increase the real GDP indicator, which will ultimately contribute to reducing the volume of debt obligations. As a priority contributing to this goal, the RA Government intends to significantly increase the volume of trade turnover[44], especially in connection with the current geopolitical situation, when Armenia, in particular, is the "gateway of Europe" for Russia, which is the main trading partner.

The overwhelming majority of scientific publications on external public debt management refer to quantitative analyzes of the latter. Despite the fact that the results of such an analysis indicate possible scenarios of debt policy pursued in the future by politicians and performers, as well as possible obstacles associated with them, nevertheless, it is necessary to conduct a qualitative analysis to interpret the effectiveness of the use of borrowed funds, and also indicate the most effective directions of using them.

However, as in many countries, in RA as well, from the point of view of universal philosophical understanding, there is still a strong need to increase the effectiveness of debt policy implementation.[45]

In the article, based on the conclusions arising from the conducted scientific research, the authors made the following accents:

[44] In 2021, major trading partners of the RA included Russia from the CIS countries (31.4% of trade turnover, compared to 30.6% of the previous year), and from the EU and other countries China (15% and 13.5%, respectively), Iran (6.0% and 5.6 %), Switzerland (4.6% and 6.6%), Germany (3.5% and 4.2%), Italy (3.4% and 3.3%), Bulgaria (2.7% and 2.4%) and the Netherlands (2.7% and 1.8%). Source: RA Ministry of Finance www.minfin.am

[45] RA GOVERNMENT DEBT BURDEN REDUCTION PROGRAM 2022-2026, p. 4

1. to introduce the need for a qualitative analysis of the external public debt management strategy in combination with the basic data of quantitative indicators;

2. the need for legislative corrections on other indicators, in particular, the ratio of domestic public debt /GDP, the ratio of domestic public debt / external public debt, as well as the establishment of maximum thresholds for the above indicators, taking as a basis the indicators recorded in previous years;

3. to increase the provision of accountability and transparency of information on the direction of use and the direction of attraction of external public debt.

4. As known, the external state debt is involved in order to finance certain investment projects. We believe that ensuring the accountability of the used funds will also help ensure that the debt funds involved in the legislation are addressed to the specific investment program.

5. Taking into account the prototypes of Eurobonds issued by RA in the international capital market in recent years and the directions of their use, it is allowed to emphasize that in the structure of the RA state debt, the debt denominated in foreign currency is a predominant part, and also the directions of use of the involved funds do not correspond to capital-creating directions.

6. We consider it necessary to emphasize that the implementation of a stimulating policy aimed at issuing and purchasing government Treasury bonds on the domestic market by the RA Government in the long term may significantly weaken the share of debt quoted in the currency existing in the structure of the RA government debt. The latter is considered quite risky, since in the context of debt management it increases the risks of refinancing and the exchange rate.

Thus, despite the fact that in 2008 the RA Government managed to overcome the challenges caused by the financial and economic crisis, since it did not have a very high level of public debt, nevertheless, in the current situation, when the debt-to-GDP ratio in 2020 was 63.5%[46], exceeding the threshold set by the RA legislation in 60%, additional global shocks caused by the current

[46] As of December 31, 2020, the debt of the RA government exceeded 60% of GDP, making 63.5%. Based on the presented RA fiscal rules, it is planned to implement fiscal consolidation, reducing the government's debt from 60% of GDP by 2026.

geopolitical situation, the irreducible high level of debt can have an extremely negative impact on the financial and economic system of the RA.

Due to the continuous growth of the state debt, the authors emphasize the urgency of additional multilateral analyses, in the context of ensuring the consistency of the decisions of the RA Government on the injection of foreign state debt and the addressability of the policy adopted and implemented by the latter[47].

The reasons for the formation of external debt in both developing and developed countries are a consequence of war, financial and economic crises, internal political conflicts, socio-economic problems, and the imperfection of the legislative framework that occurred in different historical periods.

Armenian researcher E. Hakobyan, in the framework of his dissertation for the degree of candidate of economic sciences "THE IMPACT OF STATE DEBT POLICY ON ECONOMIC GROWTH (ISSUES OF THEORY AND PRACTICE)", studying the views of theorists of different periods, distinguished two groups of theorists, the first of which has a negative attitude towards debt, and the second has a positive attitude.

As a result of the research, the following four main directions of the theory of state debt were emphasized:

1. Early classical: Hume, Smith, Ricardo believed that borrowing is not effective, since it, strengthening the state, destroys capital.

2. Late classical and new classical. Malthus, Mill believed that debt is not always ineffective if the state attracts resources that can be used effectively. Later, Adams, Bastable, Leroy-Beaulieu came to the conclusion that debt can benefit society if the funds attracted by the state are directed to investments. The new classical Barrow also showed that the economy is indifferent to how the state finances its expenses.

3. Keynesian (stabilization theory). Keynes, Lerner, Samuelson, Galbraith, Harris put forward the theory of stabilization of the state budget deficit and

---

[47] MATEVOSYAN, A. & GRIGORYAN, A. (2022). "The Philosophy of External Public Debt Management". *WISDOM*, *24*(4), 91–101. https://doi.org/10.24234/wisdom.v24i4.945 available at the following link: https://wisdomperiodical.com/index.php/wisdom/article/view/945

believed that the state should actively intervene in economic processes and regulate the economy through fiscal policy, and debt cannot harm state finances and the economy in the long run.

4. Other theories. Buchanan approached the late classical with his approaches. Friedman and Monetarists generally rejected fiscal policy as a tool for stabilizing the economy.[48]

Since the research views of theorists interested in studying the debt issue in different periods are not unified on debt policy, in this sub-question of the dissertation we have considered the main research direction not to be the discussions and approaches on the debt issue among representatives of different schools of economics, but to emphasize the principles of assessing debt sustainability, as well as the study of the "bitter experience" of countries that have overcome debt crises.

In international practice, the goals of public debt management in different countries (Brazil, Sweden, the USA, the United Kingdom) mainly coincide, but as a result of the different political and economic situations of the countries, they have differences.[49]

There are significant differences between large and small countries in terms of debt. The maximum size of the public debt of EU member states was set by the Maastricht Treaty. According to it, the public debt of member states should not exceed 60 percent of GDP.[50]

The 2007–2009 financial crisis and subsequent economic downturn in the United States led to large government deficits that accelerated the growth of the overall debt, which led to the introduction of a number of debt limits. Past experience shows that direct fiscal spending during a financial crisis, such as

---

[48] HAKOBYAN E. N., (2016). "THE IMPACT OF STATE DEBT POLICY ON ECONOMIC GROWTH (ISSUES OF THEORY AND PRACTICE)", Phd THESIS for the degree of Candidate of Economics in the specialty "General Economics", pp. 6-7, available at the following link: http://councils.ysu.am/pdf_files/015/2016/015-Eduard_Hakobyan.pdf

[49] Melikyan S., (2013). "Features of the Formation and Management of the RA State Debt", p. 7, available at the following link http://library.asue.am/books/2791.pdf

[50] Kyurumyan A., (2014). "Political decisions made in recent years regarding public debt management and their consequences", p. 4, available at the following link: https://www.osf.am/wp-content/uploads/2014/04/Debt-Managment_Artak-Kyurumyan.pdf

spending to bail out financial institutions,[51] are weakened by declining tax revenues and increased social security benefits[52]

The large burden of public debt accumulated in the world is truly worrying, as there are at least two reasons underlying the need to reduce it. The first is the need to respond to shocks: reducing the burden of public debt will provide governments with an additional opportunity to respond to domestic and external shocks if necessary. The current world is not free from such developments (secondary effects of the global crisis, instability in financial markets, geopolitical conflicts, dollar appreciation, oil price shock, low economic growth, etc.), and Armenia is no exception (decreased external demand, economic recession in its main partner Russia, devaluation of the dram, decreased investments, etc.).

However, on the other hand, the problem of reducing the debt burden is significantly complicated by such global challenges as high levels of poverty and unemployment, inequality, population aging, growth of private debt, and weak economic growth forecast for the current and near future.

The second reason is that high public debt can negatively affect economic growth, as it will create a debt overhang effect and other negative factors, since in developed countries the public debt burden has exceeded the 90% mark. In particular, according to the view of Kuman and Wu, debt above this limit begins to negatively affect economic growth, and in developing countries this negative relationship exists even at low levels of debt burden.[53]

The progressive trend of external public debt is a worrying circumstance for both economically developed and developing countries. However, the existence of external debt is not so much a concern as its maintenance within a manageable range. The memories of specialists, as well as researchers interested in the debt issue, are still fresh in the minds of the "bitter experience" of countries that have overcome debt collapses, such as Argentina, Hungary, Portugal, Ireland, Greece, and Italy. In the precedents of the debt collapses of the mentioned countries, it is

---

[51] Carmen M. Reinhardt and Kenneth S. Rogoff. (2009). "This Time is Different: Eight Centuries of Financial Folly", (*Princeton: Princeton, NJ*

[52] Austin, A. (2015). "The Debt Limit: History and Recent Increases, Analyst in Economic Policy". p. 27, available at the following link: https://sgp.fas.org/crs/misc/RL31967.pdf

[53] Kumar and Woo (2010), Cechetti, Mohanti and Zampolli (2011), Checherita and Rother (2010), and for developing countries, also the works of Presbitero (2010).

noteworthy that the "European community" played a key role in overcoming the debt crises of the mentioned European countries.[54]

Since the financial and economic crisis of 2008-2009, a progressive trend in debt indicators has been observed in the world during 2021. High public debt indicators were recorded in Belgium, France, Canada, France (see Appendix No. 1).

In 2021, Venezuela ranked second among the countries with the highest level of public debt relative to its GDP, with debt estimated at three times its GDP. Countries with the highest levels of public debt often have high levels of economic instability, but this list also includes many developed economies, such as Japan and the United States, which are notable for their high levels of national borrowing and government spending. The United States has the largest public debt in fiscal terms, while Japan has the largest relative debt of any developed economy relative to its GDP. The country's growing debt is approximately $12.5 trillion in 2021, while its GDP is only $5.1 trillion. The Japanese government currently spends about half of its total tax revenue on servicing its massive debt. Despite this, the yield on Japan's 10-year bond remains surprisingly low, below 1 percent.[55]

Thus, the burden of public debt has become a global challenge, and its reduction is a rather complex and problematic phenomenon. Historically, the ways to reduce the debt burden have been economic growth, restrictive fiscal policy, default and restructuring, inflation, financial pressures (restriction of capital flows, regulation of interest rates, etc.).

In this context, we emphasize the approach to assessing the debt of countries proposed by the Armenian researcher E. Hakobyan, according to which zone they are in: green (large debt, but large fiscal opportunities), yellow (some fiscal opportunities, but high risk of the state), or red (large debt, but lack of fiscal opportunities).[56]

---

[54] Григорян, А. (2022). "ТЕОРЕТИКО-МЕТОДИЧЕСКИЕ ОСНОВЫ УПРАВЛЕНИЯ ВНЕШНИМ ГОСУДАРСТВЕННЫМ ДОЛГОМ РА И ЗАРУБЕЖНЫЙ ОПЫТ"; *(Регион и мир, 2022, № 3), с. 129-132*
http://geopolitika.am/dir/wp-content/blogs.dir/1/files/2022_3_127_133.pdf

[55] Source: www.statista.com

[56] HAKOBYAN E. (2015). "THE BURDENS OF PUBLIC DEBT IN THE WORLD: CHALLENGES OF THE 21ST CENTURY", KNOWLEDGE, INNOVATION AND

The Greek debt crisis, the debt danger in Portugal, Ireland, and Italy, and the debt problems widely discussed in many other countries during the recent financial and economic crisis are still fresh in the minds of experts and those interested in the issue. The above proves that the issue of the size and manageability of public debt is not only relevant now, but also cannot be ignored under any circumstances.[57]

Argentina's economic crisis (1998-2002).[58] Argentina experienced the worst economic crisis in its history from 1998 to 2002. On December 23, Argentina's new President Saa officially declared a default on the government's debt.[59] The high level of public debt, the vulnerable structure and reduced volumes of exports, the lack of flexibility of the labor market, the high dependence on foreign currency borrowing and the high level of dollarization did not allow Argentina to withstand external shocks, as a result of which the economy collapsed.

Economic crisis of Hungary (2008-2009).[60] The government's misguided policies on public debt and public spending, combined with high banking system risk and global financial turmoil, plunged Hungary into a severe economic crisis in the fall of 2008, which continued into 2009. Public debt to GDP ratio rose from 66.1% at the end of 2007 to 78.4% at the end of 2009, while gross external debt rose from 103.2% at the end of 2007 to 146.2% at the end of 2009.

Greek debt crisis (2010–2018). The economic and debt crisis in Greece was the result of poor management of public finances, which occurred in particular

---

DEVELOPMENT, Proceedings of the 25th ASUE SCIENTIFIC CONFERENCE, November 11-13, pp. 169-171, available at the following link:
https://asue.am/upload/files/II_Baj._tarmacvac.pdf

[57] Григорян, А. (2022). "ТЕОРЕТИКО-МЕТОДИЧЕСКИЕ ОСНОВЫ УПРАВЛЕНИЯ ВНЕШНИМ ГОСУДАРСТВЕННЫМ ДОЛГОМ РА И ЗАРУБЕЖНЫЙ ОПЫТ"; *(Регион и мир, 2022, № 3), 127-129*
http://geopolitika.am/dir/wp-content/blogs.dir/1/files/2022_3_127_133.pdf

[58] IMF (2015). "Lessons from the Crisis in Argentina". available at the following link:https://bit.ly/3d4EVAP

[59] The exception was a portion of the government debt, which was put under structural review back in November 2001.

[60] Horvath, J. (2009). "2008 Hungarian Financial Crisis". CASE Network E-briefs. Najdeno 1. junija 2016 na spletnem naslovu: available at the following link: http://www.case-research.eu/upload/publikacja_pUUUlik/23686666_E-brief_012009%20FINAL.pdf

due to reduced capital spending, increased current spending, increased public debt, and a slowdown in GDP growth amid demand-led economic growth.

The economic collapse lasted much longer than the Great Depression in the United States in the 1930s. Public debt rose from 100% to 180% of GDP, most of which was foreign debt. On June 21, 2018, Greece's creditors agreed to extend the repayment period of loans worth about €97 billion by 10 years.[61] Greece emerged from the debt crisis on August 20, 2018.

A study of the experience of these countries allows us to notice that in all three cases, the problem of its incorrect allocation in the structure of state budget expenditures, parallel to the increase in the government debt burden, runs like a red thread.[62]

The peculiarity of the impact of the crisis in Armenia was that its primary impact, namely, panic in financial markets and the problem of liquidity of banks and other financial organizations, did not manifest itself. This was largely due to the fact that the stock market sector of the financial market was not so developed in Armenia, as well as the rather strict policy of supervision of financial institutions in Armenia was applied by the Central Bank of Armenia. However, the secondary impact of the financial and economic crisis was observed in Armenia, which affected the economy in the following 4 directions:

• a significant reduction in private transfers from abroad,

• a decrease in the prices of raw materials and especially metals in world markets,

• a decline in the demand for exports of exported goods and services due to the decline in aggregate demand in the world economy,

---

[61] Almost a third of Greece's total debt.

[62] "THE POSSIBILITY OF ECONOMIC COLLAPSE IN ARMENIA: MYTH OR REAL THREAT?", "LUYS Foundation", 2021, pages 34-47, available at the following link https://www.luys.am/img/artpic/small/5330d854e7677d361266%D5%8F%D5%B6%D5%BF%D5%A5%D5%BD%D5%A1%D5%AF%D5%A1%D5%B6%D5%AF%D5%B8%D5%AC%D5%A1%D5%BA%D5%BD--07-07-2021-edited.pdf

• a decline in the volume of investments flowing into the RA economy due to the liquidity problems of financial assets in the world economy.[63]

Emphasizing the need to assess debt sustainability, let us note that sustainability is an important characteristic of sound macroeconomic policy, but its precise definition is unclear and its assessment is even more difficult.[64]

Sustainability is a living process, consisting of a series of actions and functions that take place every day within a well-established legal framework and a well-established and functioning institutional structure. To have a good and reliable assessment of real debt sustainability, we need to assess each of the above dimensions in each country. Fiscal sustainability and debt sustainability are imperative. These two dimensions are key elements for achieving the Millennium Development Goals and for the success of the Heavily Indebted Poor Countries Initiative.[65]

According to the International Monetary Fund, although Armenia has begun to overcome the challenges in 2020, there are still some risks in the context of debt management. The risks are relatively balanced, although uncertainty remains high.[66]

When assessing the performance of public debt management and developing a medium-term debt management strategy, the question of how the debt structure is managed is of key importance. When assessing debt sustainability, the long-term sustainability of debt is important, which depends on both the size and

---

[63] Sargsyan, K., (2016). "Issues of Increasing the Efficiency of State Anti-Crisis Policy" Yerevan: "Science" Publishing House of the NAS of the Republic of Armenia, pp. 282-283

[64] Wyplosz, Ch. (2007). "Debt Sustainability Assessment: The IMF Approach and Alternatives," *IHEID Working Papers 03-2007, Economics Section, The Graduate Institute of International Studies.,* available at the following link:
https://ideas.repec.org/p/gii/giihei/heiwp03-2007.html

[65] Foncerrada, L. (2005). "Public debt sustainability. Notes on debt sustainability, development of a domestic governmet securities market and financial risks", *Análisis Económico, vol. XX, núm. 44, segundo cuatrimestre, p. 11,* available at the following link:
https://www.redalyc.org/pdf/413/41304409.pdf

[66] IMF (2021). "Republic of Armenia: 2021 Article IV Consultation, Fourth and Fifth Reviews Under the Stand-By Arrangement, and Request for Waiver of Nonobservance of Performance Criterion and Monetary Policy Consultation Clause-Press Release"; *Staff Report; and Statement by the Executive Director for the Republic of Armenia",* available at the following link:https://www.imf.org/en/Publications/CR/Issues/2021/12/21/Republic-of-Armenia-2021-Article-IV-Consultation-Fourth-and-Fifth-Revies-Under-the-Stand-511248

structure of the debt. Naturally, the size and structure of the debt are interrelated, therefore public debt management must be consistent with the fiscal environment that ensures the sustainability of that debt.[67]

The overwhelming majority of scientific publications on external public debt management are focused on quantitative analyses. Although the results of such analyses indicate possible scenarios for future debt policy pursued by policymakers and implementers, approximating the possible obstacles associated with them, it is nevertheless necessary to conduct qualitative analyses to establish the ensured effectiveness of the debt resources involved, as well as to predict the most effective directions for their use.[68]

From the perspective of increasing the efficiency of external public debt management, the mechanism of a separate debt management "office" or "agency institute" is applicable in international practice. Studies of international practice allow us to note that separate debt management agencies are mainly developed countries that have effectively functioning domestic capital markets.

The proposal to launch a separate debt management agency in the Republic of Armenia will contribute to ensuring the targeting and efficiency of external loans attracted in the future, assessing the economic growth ensured at the expense of the attracted funds, as well as increasing the accountability and transparency of the attracted funds, at the same time, it will provide an opportunity to involve specialists from the ministries of finance, economy, the central bank, government members, scientific research institutions, as well as the academic community.

The localization of the agency institute of public debt management in the Republic of Armenia will contribute to the measurability of economic growth ensured as a result of the use of funds attracted from external sources. The indicators of the volume of the external public debt of the Republic of Armenia and GDP growth recorded in the last three years indicate that GDP growth in dram terms has almost twice exceeded the indicators recorded in the previous 10 years

---

[67] Bayadyan A. H., Markosyan H. A. (2015). "The problems of public debt management and ways to solve them in the Republic of Armenia" Yerevan. "Science" Publishing House of the National Academy of Sciences of the Republic of Armenia, pp. 58-59

[68] Григорян А., (2022). "ТЕОРЕТИКО-МЕТОДИЧЕСКИЕ ОСНОВЫ УПРАВЛЕНИЯ ВНЕШНИМ ГОСУДАРСТВЕННЫМ ДОЛГОМ РА И ЗАРУБЕЖНЫЙ ОПЫТ", Регион и мир, 2022, № 2, с. 127-133, https://cyberleninka.ru/article/n/teoretiko-metodicheskie-osnovy-upravleniya-vneshnim-gosudarstvennym-dolgom-ra-i-zarubezhnyy-opyt

(in 2013, the gross domestic product of the Republic of Armenia expressed in market prices amounted to 4,555,638.2 million drams, and in 2022 - 8,496,777.9 million drams).[69]

Summarizing the main approaches to studying the international practice of debt management agencies, we have conducted an approximation of advantages, disadvantages, opportunities, and risks for the purpose of localization in Armenia, the results of which are presented in the graph below:

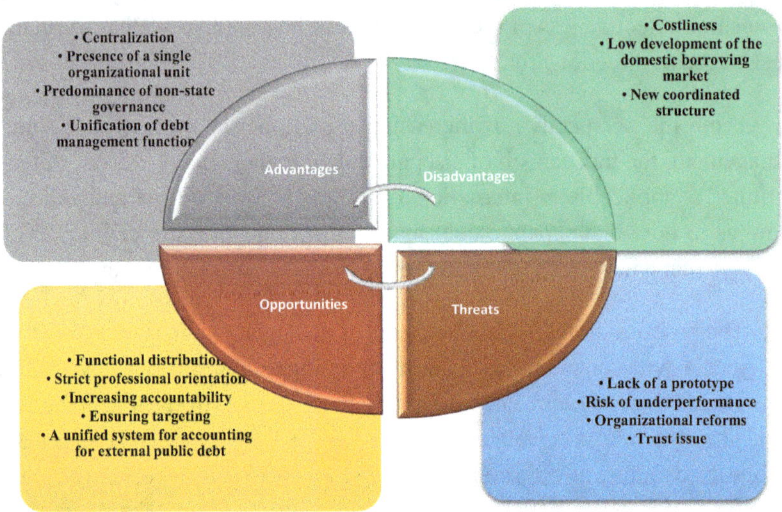

Chart 1. Results of the SWOT analysis of the operation of a debt management agency in Armenia

Debt management agencies exist in Belgium, Greece, the Netherlands, and Slovakia. In a number of countries, the agency's functions are assigned to state treasury institutions, such as Portugal. As international experience shows, in most of the countries studied, debt management is carried out jointly by ministries of finance and debt management agencies/institutions (see Appendix 2).

Summarizing this sub-question of the research, let us note that the results of the study of foreign debt management, financing experience, and discussion of precedents of countries facing debt crises in order to improve external public debt management, we believe that the manifestation of strict consistency by the RA

[69] Data: Statistical Committee of the Republic of Armenia www.armstat.am

Government in increasing the level of measurability and accountability of the effectiveness of using external borrowed funds attracted from the perspective of increasing the efficiency of RA public debt management, deserve key attention. As a result, our proposal to launch a separate public debt management agency in the RA will allow the formation of a unified public debt management system of the RA, which will contribute to the improvement of RA external public debt management.

1.3 The Philosophy of Public Debt Management in Recent Years. Evidence from Armenia, Georgia and Russia

When defining external public debt, authors refer to the legislative provisions of their countries on debt. In this context, we can highlight the RA Law "On Public Debt" adopted on May 26, 2008, which gave legal form to debt relations.

In the RA Law "On Public Debt", external public debt is defined as the sum of debt obligations assumed on behalf of the Republic of Armenia and the Central Bank towards non-residents of the Republic of Armenia and foreign states and existing at a certain point in time.[70]

There are various ways to attract external borrowed funds, such as loans from cooperating countries, loans from reputable international organizations, etc. Both developing and developed countries act as debtor countries. As a result, debt relations have currently become an inseparable companion of globalization.

The RA Law "On State Debt" defines the following sources of attracting external state debt:

1) loans and credits from foreign states, international organizations, and multilateral lending institutions.

2) loans and credits from non-resident individuals and legal entities.

---

[70] The RA Law "On State Debt", Article 2, is available at the following link: https://www.arlis.am/documentview.aspx?docid=49156

3) state treasury bonds and bonds issued in foreign currency acquired by non-residents.

4) external state guarantees.[71]

Depending on the problems facing the country, the goals of the economic policy being implemented and those to be implemented in the future, as well as the strategic priorities of public debt management, the goals of raising debt funds are diverse.

The Law on Public Debt in Armenia sets out the following primary goals for raising public debt:

1) financing the state budget deficit and ensuring current liquidity.

2) supporting the balance of payments and replenishing reserves.

3) maintaining and developing the domestic public debt market.[72]

The increasing debt burden forces policymakers to create debt management tools through various mechanisms, guided by certain principles.

In Armenia, a strategic three-year program is being developed for the purpose of public debt management, which reflects the government's debt indicators and the assessment of possible risks, and is included in the medium-term public expenditure program.

In Armenia, public debt management is carried out by the Ministry of Finance of the Republic of Armenia and the Central Bank of the Republic of Armenia, with respect to its debt.[73]

During the development of the debt management strategy, the Ministry of Finance of the Republic of Armenia, through a priori analysis, identifies obstacles and potential risks that may hinder the effective management of debt. During the development of multi-faceted studies and program provisions, the Ministry of Finance of the Republic of Armenia applies the results of the best practices in public debt management, as well as debt management approaches and toolkits

---

[71] See the same source, Article 20:

[72] See the same source, Article 8

[73] See the same source, Article 11, 12

developed by reputable organizations in the field. The results of the study allow assessing the indicators of the public debt of the Republic of Armenia in the context of the impact of the most risky shocks.

Taking into account the strategies of the public debt management of the Republic of Armenia in previous years, we can state that in strategic assessments, the size of the external debt is the dominant part of the public debt portfolio, which determines the most vulnerable exchange rate and interest rate risks to the debt. At the same time, the public debt of the Republic of Armenia is assessed as sensitive to refinancing, operational and non-market risks.

The development of the RA public debt management strategy is based on the overarching goal of ensuring maximum satisfaction of financial needs through an optimal expenditure policy, taking into account both the potential of the domestic lending market and the ways of relying on external borrowing.

The objectives of the RA Government's debt management have been set:

1) formation of the optimal structure of the government's debt, taking into account potential risks,

2) coordination of public debt management and monetary policies,

The RA public debt management is carried out in accordance with the principles of transparency, accountability, predictability and publicity.[74]

In order to support public debt management in low-income countries in the context of the recent financial crisis, the IMF and World Bank staffs have developed and proposed certain tools that are combined into a single comprehensive system consisting of 3 main components.[75]

1. A Medium-Term Debt Management Strategy (MTDS) that the Government will implement to achieve the desired structure of government debt in the medium term. The latter will also include the Government's preference for the risk-cost ratio and will be consistent with long-term debt sustainability.

---

[74] RA Law "On State Debt", Articles 8, 9, 10.

[75] IMF and World Bank. (2009). "Managing Public Debt: Formulating Strategies and Strengening Institutional Capacity". p. 8

2. A Debt Management Implementation Assessment Toolkit (DeMPA), which assesses the strengths and weaknesses of the institutional arrangements for public debt management in a given country.

3. Targeted capacity building and technical assistance that can be used when a country needs assistance on a specific debt management issue.

In this sub-question of the book, we have examined the strategic directions of public debt management in the Republic of Armenia's trading partners, the Russian Federation and Georgia, as a result of which certain commonalities are observed with the current public debt management strategies of the Republic of Armenia and Georgia, taking into account the similar macroeconomic indicators and structural features of public debt recorded by the two countries in recent years.

During the study, almost the same picture is observed in our and Georgia's macroeconomic indicators (in particular, in terms of debt structure, economic growth rate), but in the case of the Russian Federation, the picture is different.

As shown by the 2021 data published by the Ministry of Finance of Georgia,[76] in the structure of public debt, 80 percent is external debt and 20 percent is domestic debt, while the data published in 2022 shows an improvement of 5 percentage points in the overall public debt portfolio, with external public debt accounting for 75 percent and domestic public debt accounting for 25 percent.[77]

The Government of Georgia's Debt Management Strategy for 2023-2026 includes:

➢ Description of the public debt portfolio.

➢ Strategic directions for general government debt management.

---

[76] Ministry of Finance of Georgia, (2021), "External Government debt portfolio (31 Dec 2021) represents 80% of the total Government debt", available at the following link: https://www.mof.ge/en/4409

[77] Ministry of Finance of Georgia. "General Government Debt Management Strategy 2023-2026", pp. 2, 9, available at the following link:
https://www.mof.ge/images/File/sagvalebi/2023/20-01-2023/1/Government%20Debt%20Management%20Strategy%202023-2026%20-%20Presentation.pdf

➢ Target indicators.

Moreover, the strategic directions for government debt management include:

1. Maintaining a safe level of the government's net debt to GDP ratio,

2. Increasing the share of debt denominated in lari in the public debt portfolio,

3. Increasing focus on external loans aimed at development,

4. Optimization of the costs and risks of the government's general debt portfolio,

5. Development of the treasury securities market.

The "Monetary Policy Guide for 2020–2022" of the Central Bank of the Russian Federation, which is the main trading partner of the Republic of Armenia, makes it clear that over the forecast horizon, the Russian Federation Government will implement a fiscal policy that supports the dynamics of economic activity.[78]

Turning to the Russian Federation's public debt strategy, it should be noted that there is a possibility of reaching the 20% of GDP threshold, which is considered a safety margin and is enshrined in the Russian Federation's State Program "Public Finance Management and Regulation of Financial Markets".

The Russian Federation's debt-to-GDP ratio is 16.5 percent. For developing countries, the debt level should not exceed 50% of GDP. According to IMF recommendations, the Russian Federation has a 3-fold safety margin, which indicates that there are no problems with public debt management and high solvency in the current period.

The structure of the Russian Federation's public debt is assessed as quite optimal from the currency risk perspective, since the structure of the Russian Federation's public debt is dominated by debt obligations denominated in the national currency - more than 75%, which corresponds to the ratio of the share of

[78] Central Bank of the Russian Federation. "Monetary Policy Guidelines for 2020–2022", available at the following link: https://www.cbr.ru/eng/publ/ondkp/on_2020_2022/page/

the Russian Federation's public domestic debt in the total measure of public debt (65% and more) set by the state program.

The actual structure of the Russian Federation's public debt indicates effective management of public debt and low currency risks. Unlike Russia, in developing countries, as a rule, a significant part of the public debt structure is occupied by external debt. For example, Brazil, Korea, India and Belarus have large external debt, which indicates that these countries have low debt sustainability.

The external public debt of the Russian Federation mainly consists of liabilities on government securities denominated in foreign currency (75%). It should be noted that the Ministry of Finance of the Russian Federation periodically buys back existing Eurobonds and issues new ones on more favorable terms for the state, including in terms of reducing the coupon rate in order to maintain the liquidity of the market for these securities.

The repurchase of previously issued bonds by the Ministry of Finance of the Russian Federation in recent years not only reduces debt servicing costs, but also minimizes market and refinancing risks, which indicates the effective management of Russia's external public debt.[79]

Policy measures aimed at the development of the Russian financial market, which are jointly implemented and planned by the Russian Government and the Central Bank of Russia, are described in detail in the Guidelines for the Development of the Russian Financial Market in 2019-2021 and the Draft Guidelines for the Development of the Russian Financial Market in 2022-2024.[80]

---

[79] Atanasovska, Yu.V.; Sanginova, L.D.; Balynin, I.V. (2020), "State Debt Management in the Russian Federation in Modern Socio-Economic Conditions" *Advances in Economics, Business and Management Research, volume 138 2nd International Scientific and Practical Conference "Modern Management Trends and the Digital Economy: from Regional Development to Global Economic Growth" (MTDE 2020),*
https://doi.org/10.2991/aebmr.k.200502.212 pp. 1279-1280, available at the following link: https://www.atlantis-press.com/proceedings/mtde-20/125939842

[80] The draft Guidelines for the Development of the Russian Financial Market in 2022–2024 were published on the Bank of Russia website on 28 July 2021, available at the following link: http://www.cbr.ru/s/2569

Policy measures aimed at financial market development mainly have a long-term impact.[81]

In this sub-question of the survey, we also examined what external debt indicators have been recorded in Russia and Georgia in recent years.

Russia's external debt reached $357.9 billion in March 2023, compared to $380.5 billion in the previous quarter. Moreover, the external debt indicator reached its highest level of $732.8 billion in June 2014, and its record low of $146.3 billion in December 2001.

In Russia's latest reports, the current account recorded a surplus of $5.2 billion in May 2023. Foreign direct investment (FDI) increased by $795.1 million in December 2022. Russia's direct investment abroad increased by $7.1 billion in December 2022, while foreign portfolio investment decreased by $604.0 million in December 2022. The country's nominal GDP in March 2023 was $494.7 billion.[82]

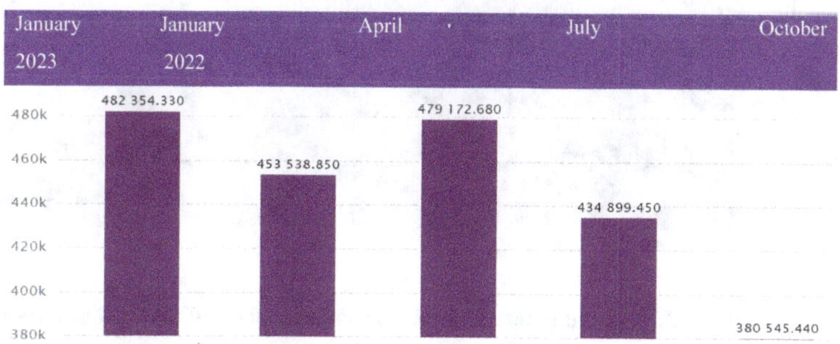

Figure 1. Russian external public debt in 2022 in US dollars[83]

[81] Central Bank of the Russian Federation. "Monetary Policy Guidelines for 2022–2024". pp. 16-17, available at the following link:
https://www.cbr.ru/content/document/file/126065/on_project_2022(2023-2024)_eng.pdf

[82] Russia External Debt, available at the following link:
https://www.ceicdata.com/en/indicator/russia/external-debt

[83] Source: WWW.CEICDATA.COM | CEIC Data

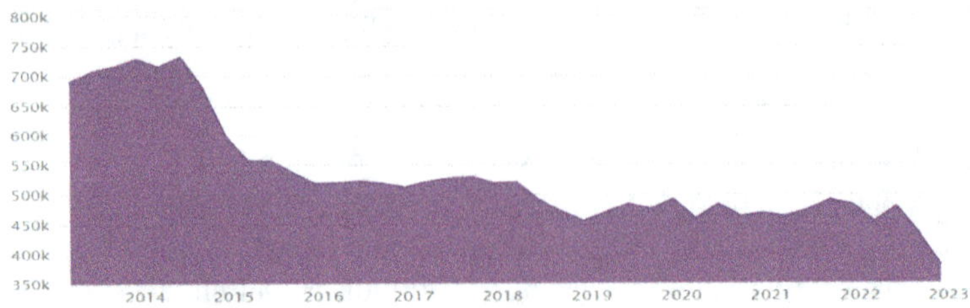

Figure 2. Russian external public debt in 2014-2023 in US dollars[84]

In 2022, the Russian Federation's external public debt amounted to 17.0% of the country's nominal GDP, compared to 26.3% in the previous year. There was a certain increase in the public debt/GDP ratio, in particular, in March 2023, public debt amounted to 15.5% of nominal GDP, compared to 14.9% in the previous quarter.[85]

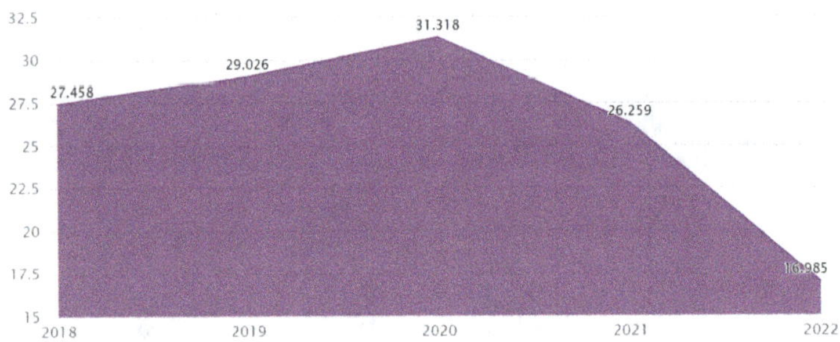

Figure 3. Russian external debt / GDP ratio 2018-2022 in US dollars[86]

Georgia's external debt reached $23.5 billion in December 2022, compared to $22.2 billion in the previous quarter. The external debt peaked in December 2022 at $23.5 billion, and reached a record low of $2.2 billion in September 2000. In Georgia's latest reports, the current account recorded a deficit of $538.5 million in December 2022. Foreign direct investment (FDI) increased by $324.7 million in December 2022. In December 2022, Georgia's direct investment abroad increased by $106.2 million, while foreign portfolio investment decreased by

[84] Source: WWW.CEICDATA.COM | CEIC Data

[85] What was Russia's Government Debt: % of GDP in Mar 2023? available at the following link: https://www.ceicdata.com/datapage/en/indicator/russia/government-debt--of-nominal-gdp

[86]Source: WWW.CEICDATA.COM | CEIC Data

$41.8 million in December 2022. The country's nominal GDP in December 2022 was $7.5 billion.[87]

Georgia's external debt in 2022 amounted to 94.8% of the country's nominal GDP, compared to 117.8% in the previous year. Moreover, the external debt/GDP ratio reached its highest level in history in December 2020, amounting to 131.5%.[88] Georgia's public debt amounted to 37.5% of the country's nominal GDP in March 2023, compared to 39.7% in the previous quarter.[89]

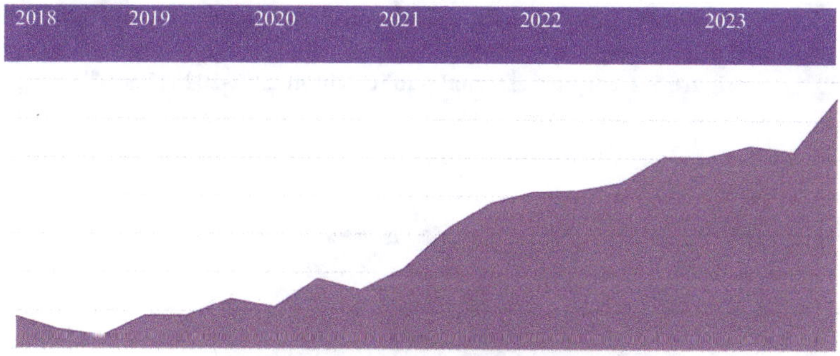

Figure 4. Georgia's external public debt in 2014-2023 in USD[90]

[87] Georgia External Debt, available at the following link:
https://www.ceicdata.com/datapage/en/indicator/georgia/external-debt

[88] Georgia External Debt: % of GDP
https://www.ceicdata.com/datapage/en/indicator/georgia/external-debt--of-nominal-gdp

[89] Georgia Government Debt: % of GDP
https://www.ceicdata.com/datapage/en/indicator/georgia/government-debt--of-nominal-gdp

[90] Source: WWW.CEICDATA.COM | CEIC Data

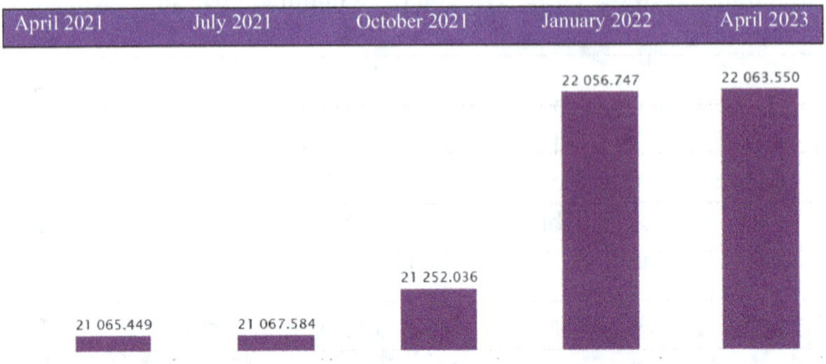

Figure 5. Georgia's external public debt in 2022-2023 (USD)[91]

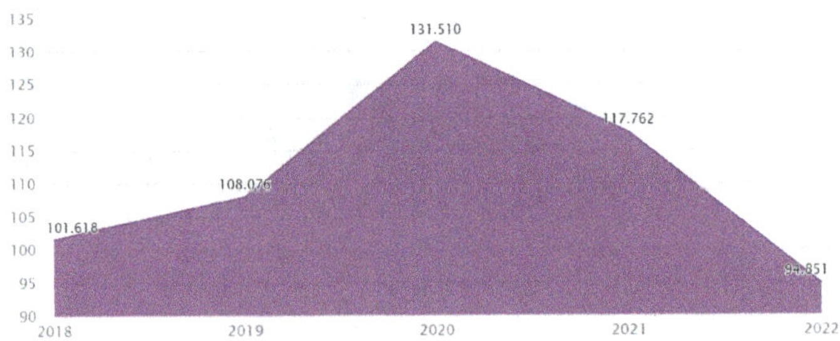

Figure 6. Georgia's external debt / GDP ratio 2018-2022 in US dollars[92]

Summarizing the results of the study of the strategic mechanisms of the debt policies of the main trading partners of the Republic of Armenia in this subsection of the book, from the perspective of improving the efficiency of the management of the Republic of Armenia's external public debt, we emphasize the need for legislative fixation of the safety margin of expenses for debt servicing and repayment (as, for example, in the partner Russia, 2-3 percent is set), which will make it possible to make the potential for servicing the debt burden involved more measurable. As a comparison, in 2021, the expenses for servicing the debt of the Republic of Armenia will amount to 2.7 percent of GDP, and in 2023, according to forecasts, the funds allocated to interest payments on the public debt will amount to about 272.1 billion drams, that is, about 10.5% of the budget expenditures for 2023.

[91]Source: WWW.CEICDATA.COM | CEIC Data

[92]Source: WWW.CEICDATA.COM | CEIC Data

CHAPTER 2. FEATURES OF EXTERNAL PUBLIC DEBT MANAGEMENT IN THE REPUBLIC OF ARMENIA

2.1 Discussion of approaches to the formation, assessment and management of external public debt. Cases from Armenia

Economic theory offers very few operational guidelines for determining the optimal debt level. There is no precise definition of the concept of "safe debt", and therefore there is no clear system for its assessment.

International financial organizations have developed threshold indicators for assessing debt sustainability (external debt GNI/GDP, external debt GNI/exports, external debt service/exports). Widely used threshold indicators are conditional indicators of the external debt situation and only allow one to orient oneself as to what is an acceptable level of debt. The lower the actual indicators are from the threshold, the lower the risks of the country getting into a debt crisis. However, it should be noted that these indicators do not cover all aspects of the country's debt situation. It is necessary to take into account the specifics of the borrowing country, in particular: economic potential, external economic opportunities, fiscal, budgetary, and monetary policies.[93]

Public debt sustainability is a necessary condition for macroeconomic stability and long-term economic growth. However, to be considered sustainable, the government must service its debt without declaring insolvency, renegotiating debt terms, or restructuring debt, as well as without imposing unrealistically high pressures on economic policy.

Regardless of the debt and its service burden, the RA government has been able to service the RA public debt on time and in full over the past decade. However, this circumstance is not sufficient for full judgments about sustainability. To ensure sustainability, it is necessary to identify all possible risks

[93] Movsisyan, Sh., (2018). "Problems of Debt Security of the RA Economy", ECONOMY AND SOCIETY DEVELOPMENT. Challenges and Opportunities of the 21st Century. Proceedings of the 27th ASUE Conference / ASUE. Economist, 2018, p. 59, available at the following link: https://asue.am/upload/files/Gitajoxovi-nyuter.pdf

and sources of vulnerability in order to visualize the behavior of the debt in the event of the emergence of these risks.

The RA Government Debt Management Strategy clarifies the debt raising policy, including benchmarks for government debt management, identifies and assesses the risks associated with government debt management, and outlines the principles, objectives, and measures to be implemented under which fiscal sustainability will not be jeopardized.[94]

In this subsection of the study, the results of the analysis of the sustainability of the RA public debt, based on the MAC DSA (Debt sustainability analysis for market-access countries) methodology of two reputable financial institutions, the International Monetary Fund and the World Bank, widely used in international practice, served as the basis for the proposed new approach to improving the management of the RA external public debt. The MAC DSA model is a standardized system for the multi-faceted analysis of medium-term risks, which can be fully applied in the analysis of the sustainability of the Armenian debt.[95]

Armenia meets all the necessary conditions for using the model, in particular:

1. Has significant and stable access to international capital markets. In 2013, 2015, 2019, 2020, tranches of Eurobonds of 700 and 500 million USD were successfully issued,[96] the steady downward trend in yields on these bonds in the secondary market and the sovereign ratings received from international organizations Moody's and Fitch reflect the availability of such access.[97]

2021 was special in that three highly reputable international rating agencies - Moody's, Fitch, and S&P Poor's - simultaneously gave a positive assessment to the economic policies pursued by the government, confirming their reliability. This is also important because these assessments were carried out during the

---

[94] "RA GOVERNMENT DEBT MANAGEMENT STRATEGIC PLAN FOR 2022-2024" p. 3, available at the following link: https://minfin.am/hy/page/partqi_razmavarutyun/

[95] RA Ministry of Finance. (2019). "Analysis of the Sustainability of the Government Debt of the Republic of Armenia", p. 19

[96] In 2024, a new Eurobond issuance is planned on the international capital market, again to repay the previously assumed obligation, which, although it will not constitute an additional burden on the state budget of the Republic of Armenia, will not create additional value either.

[97] RA Ministry of Finance, (2019). "Analysis of the Sustainability of the Government Debt of the Republic of Armenia", p. 20

period of overcoming the major challenges of 2020 - the consequences of the coronavirus and the war, and confirmed the effectiveness of the economic programs implemented by the Armenian government and the positive assessment of these reputable organizations regarding the prospects for macroeconomic stability.[98]

2. The share of preferential loans in the government debt portfolio has a decreasing trend. We can consider the decrease in the share of preferential loans in the structure of external public debt as both a positive and a negative trend. In the context of GDP growth rates, the average income level of the population is increasing, and the Republic of Armenia is already attracting loans on market terms. On the other hand, we can emphasize that currently there are almost no cheap loans. The large share of loans attracted on preferential terms in the debt structure indicates the low income level of the population and the low development of the country.

3. The macroeconomic statistics necessary for the model are available in the publications of the Statistical Committee of the Republic of Armenia and the Central Bank of the Republic of Armenia, and the indicators related to the state budget and government debt are available in the statistical bulletins of the Ministry of Finance of the Republic of Armenia and in the public debt reports.

4. The list of countries with access to the market is given by the organizations developing the debt sustainability analysis model.[99]

Due to the economic shock caused by the COVID-19 pandemic and the consequences of the Second Artsakh War, the response to the latter with a stimulating fiscal policy, and the financing of additional state budget expenditure requirements, the debt burden of the RA government increased sharply in 2020, exceeding the 60% threshold, amounting to 63.5%, after the fiscal consolidation recorded in 2018-2019.[100] The government debt/GDP ratio increased by 13.4

---

[98] RA Ministry of Finance, (2022). “The Minister of Finance presented the draft state budget of the Republic of Armenia for 2022 in the National Assembly”, available at the following link: https://minfin.am/hy/content/finansneri_nakhararn_azh-um_nerkayacrel_e_hh_2022t_petakan_byujei_nakhagitsy/#sthash.RmjnyEWx.dpbs

[99] RA Ministry of Finance, (2019). "Analysis of the Sustainability of the Government Debt of the Republic of Armenia", p. 20

[100] MATEVOSYAN, A., & GRIGORYAN, A. (2023). “NEW SOLUTIONS OF PUBLIC DEBT MANAGEMENT IN THE CONTEXT OF DEBT INSTRUMENT SELECTION”. «I Международное книжное издание стран Содружество Независимых Государств /

percentage points, driven mainly by the economic downturn and exchange rate depreciation, each contributing 3.9 percentage points. The primary balance contributed 2.7 percentage points, while the real interest rate contributed 1.7 percentage points.

Given the government debt/GDP ratio recorded in 2020, the fiscal consolidation envisaged by the RA fiscal rules has started in 2021, as a result of which the government debt/GDP ratio will be below the 60% government debt threshold in 2023, and will approach the 50% GDP threshold by 2026.[101]

The decrease in the RA government debt/GDP ratio to 46.7 percent in 2022, as projected in the medium-term expenditure program, occurred at the expense of the secured 12.6 percent economic growth.

As a result of the debt sustainability analysis using the MAC DSA model, according to the parameters defined by the model methodology, the necessary level of depth of study regarding the RA government debt was assessed as subject to in-depth study.[102]

«ЛУЧШИЙ НАУЧНЫЙ СОТРУДНИК - 2023»: I международная книжная коллекция научно-педагогических работников – ISBN 978-601-341-358-7, Астана, 2023 г., с. 38-42

[101] Ministry of Finance of the Republic of Armenia, (2021). "TAXO-BUDGETARY POLICY OF THE RA FOR 2022-2024", p. 17, available at the following link: https://minfin.am/website/images/files/%20%20%202022-2024.docx

[102] RA Ministry of Finance, (2019). "Analysis of the Sustainability of the Government Debt of the Republic of Armenia", pp. 24-25

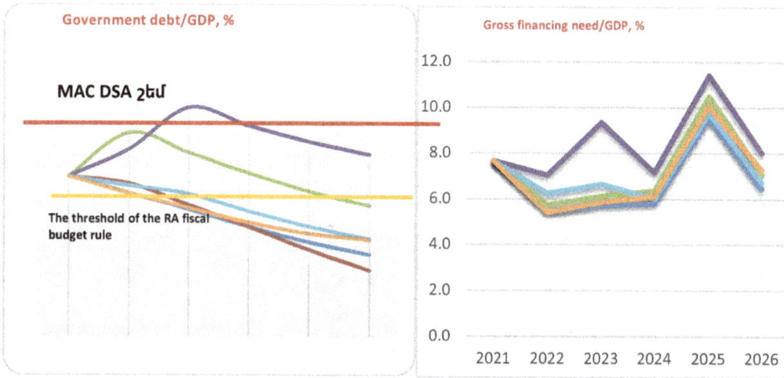

Figure 7. Stress tests of the RA Government's debt and gross financing needs[103]

Summarizing the results of the study of the assessment of the RA public debt management using the MAC DSA model, we can note that in recent years, a trend of increasing domestic debt resources has been noticeable in the financing of the RA public debt, which is positively assessed from the point of view of neutralizing foreign exchange risks, as well as reducing the share of debt assumed towards non-residents.

Summarizing the results of the study conducted in this subsection of the study, we note that the current level of the RA government debt/GDP indicator, in the context of the RA fiscal rules, makes it necessary to implement specific actions, since it exceeded 60%, the threshold assessed as marginal from the point of view of the current capabilities of the RA economy. Additional risks for the public debt are caused by the trend of increasing weighted average interest rates and debt service burden, which is also combined with the growth of the private sector's external debt and increases the vulnerability of the economy to shocks. This situation necessitates the adoption and implementation in the medium term of a fiscal consolidation policy in line with the fiscal rules of the Republic of Armenia.[104]

[103] Ministry of Finance of the Republic of Armenia, (2021) "TAXO-BUDGETARY POLICY OF THE RA FOR 2022-2024", p. 41, available at the following link https://minfin.am/website/images/files/%20%20%202022-2024.docx

[104] Matevosyan, A., Grigoryan, A. (2021). "Assessment of the analysis of the sustainability of the RA public debt according to the MAC DSA methodology of the International Monetary Fund", *"ADVANCE RESEARCH JOURNAL OF MULTIDISCIPLINARY DISCOVERIES" I Vol.68 I Issue-1 I Chapter-1 E-ISSN : 2456-1045,* available at the following

2.2 Risks of external public debt management and specifics of external liability fulfillment in the medium term. RA developments

The fiscal policies implemented by the Government of the Republic of Armenia in 2016-2018 were restrictive, focusing on ensuring the sustainability of the Government of the Republic of Armenia's debt, while at the same time targeting the restoration of economic growth and ensuring macroeconomic stability.

In 2020, fiscal policy was expansionary to counteract the economic shock caused by the pandemic. After 2021, fiscal policy had a neutral orientation, while simultaneously promoting long-term economic growth by increasing the share of public investment.[105]

In order to keep the main risks of the RA government's debt management within manageable limits and, in particular, to reduce the risk of high exchange rates, the development of the domestic public debt market and the increase in the weight of debt in Armenian drams in the government's debt are considered as strategic objectives.[106]

As a result of the COVID-19 pandemic, the global economy suffered heavy losses, declining by 3.3%, while the decline in our main partner Russia amounted to 3.1%. 2020 was a negative year for Armenia due to the severe consequences of the Second Artsakh War, as a result of which the RA economy experienced a decline of 7.4%. However, since 2021, the wounds of the deep economic recession in the RA began to heal. The pace of economic recovery in the RA continued in 2022. It is noteworthy that the 5.7% economic growth recorded in 2021 was still not a sufficient indicator to overcome the negative effects of the 7.4% economic recession in 2020.[107]

However, in 2022, Armenia recorded certain economic successes, largely due to the "Russian factor", which, of course, was fateful for ensuring double-digit economic growth in Armenia. From this perspective, we can emphasize that

---

link:http://www.journalresearchijf.com/wp-content/uploads/FM-V68-I1-C1-DEC-2021-PP-01-09.pdf?fbclid=IwAR3RyDu0ls8P9TrJDN4X6-mvWTOd812twXYK_P4uj-RkP9O7zEGI9mjKKYU

105 "The RA Government's Strategic Debt Management Program for 2021-2023", p. 12, available at the following link: https://minfin.am/hy/page/partqi_razmavarutyun/

106 See the same place, p.21

107 Data: Statistical Committee of the Republic of Armenia www.armstat.am

in the first half of 2022 alone, Armenia's economic growth increased by 11% compared to the same period last year, with the record increase recorded in June. Naturally, many factors contributed to Armenia's economic growth, in particular:

1. The unprecedented inflow of transfers and Russians arriving in Armenia gave a boost to economic growth.

2. Banks that tripled their profits. When the flow of Russians to Armenia increased after the Russian-Ukrainian war, banks began to raise their prices for their services one after another, for example, for money transfers and cash withdrawal services.

3. The booming restaurants and hotels, trade sector and other services gave a boost to economic growth. In the first half of 2022, 43% of tourists arriving in Armenia were from Russia. A 30.3% increase was recorded in the information and communication sector. In general, growth is observed in almost all sectors of services in 2022.

3. Construction has also become more active (construction contributed to growth by 1.41 percentage points).[108]

Thus, in the first half of 2022, 588,731 tourists arrived in Armenia from abroad. This number has increased 2.4 times compared to the same half of 2021. As a result, we can consider the driving force of the economic growth recorded at the end of 2022 to be the record inflow of funds from Russian tourists to Armenia.

Although the "Russian factor" provides temporary positive economic results, certain risks are nevertheless tangible. If the situation in Russia stabilizes and Russians who moved to Armenia return to their homeland, the Armenian economy will suffer significantly. In other words, the foundations for growth are not long-term.

In studies on the management of the state debt of the Republic of Armenia, ensuring the consolidation of monetary and fiscal policies is of key importance. In particular, Armenian researcher G. Petrosyan, in his dissertation for the degree of Candidate of Economics on the topic "External Shocks and Problems of Ensuring Macroeconomic Stability in the Republic of Armenia", referring to the RA economy, noted that monetary policy alone is not sufficient in reducing

[108] Hegyan, S., (2023). "13% economic growth recorded in the second quarter, mainly provided by trade and services", available at the following link: https://hetq.am/hy/article/147571

vulnerability to external shocks, and the response of fiscal policy is also important.[109]

It is noteworthy that although the inflation factors in 2020-2021 were mainly global in nature, various central banks around the world delayed their policy response, considering the current inflation to be a "temporary" phenomenon. The main goal of monetary policy is to anchor inflation expectations and prevent inflation acceleration in the face of "temporary" inflation factors.

It can be noted that Armenia was one of the first in the world to start raising interest rates in December 2020, anticipating an acceleration in inflation. As a result, the timely and necessary response allowed the Central Bank of Armenia to have a more restrained acceleration of inflation by raising the interest rate less.[110]

Fiscal policy should be aimed at reducing the government debt burden and promoting long-term economic growth. Under conditions of high economic growth, it is planned to smoothly reduce the government debt burden, bringing it to 52.1% of GDP by 2026. Reducing the debt burden by about 8 percentage points from the threshold of 60% set by fiscal rules will allow creating a "fiscal space" or accumulating the necessary reserve of resilience that is vital for responding to potential shocks.[111]

In the medium-term forecast horizon, it is planned to implement a policy of improving the structure of state budget expenditures, as a result of which the share of state budget capital expenditures in GDP will increase significantly. In order to contribute to ensuring high rates of economic growth, it is planned to increase the share of capital expenditures in GDP in 2022-2026, bringing it to around 4.8% in 2024, and to 6.1% by 2026. It is planned to maintain a stable level of current primary expenditures relative to GDP, ensuring stabilization of the current

[109] Petrosyan, G., (2018). "External Shocks and Problems of Ensuring Macroeconomic Stability in the Republic of Armenia", Dissertation No. Г.00.02 for the degree of Candidate of Economics in the specialty "Economics and Management of the Economy, Its Sectors", pp. 122-123

[110] CBA "Inflation Report/1", "Monetary Policy Program Implementation Report for the 4th Quarter of 2021", pp. 36-38, available at the following link:
https://www.cba.am/Storage/AM/downloads/parberakan/DVQ/Monetary%20overview_I_2022.pdf

[111] "Medium-Term State Expenditure Program of the Republic of Armenia for 2022-2024", pp. 22-24, available at the following link:
https://minfin.am/hy/page/petakan_mijnazhamket_tsakhseri_tsragre/

primary expenditures/GDP ratio at around 20% in 2022-2026. The latter, however, implies the implementation of current expenditures in excess of those envisaged by fiscal rules, since current primary expenditures calculated in accordance with fiscal rules will have a decreasing trend relative to GDP. Therefore, for the implementation of this scenario, it is necessary to make certain changes to the legislative regulations of fiscal rules, creating an opportunity to increase the current expenditures in the context of high economic growth and high tax revenues (education, healthcare, defense expenditures, and etc.).[112]

Summarizing the results of the study in this subsection, we note that, according to the results of the analysis of the costs and risks of the RA government's debt portfolio, the debt portfolio is most susceptible to the impact of exchange rate risk. For this reason, the RA government considers the continuous development of the state treasury bond market and the increase in the share of dram debt due to the increase in the volume of borrowing from the domestic market to be a priority. In this context, we also emphasize that in 2023-2025 it is planned to increase the share of deficit financing at the expense of domestic net borrowed funds and ensure at least a 30% share of domestic debt in the RA government's debt structure.

2.3 Comparative analysis of economic growth and government debt indicators in the EAEU countries: Regional developments and EU trends

In this subsection of the study, we considered the period from 2009 to the present day as the period of study of the behavior of the state debt of the Republic of Armenia, based on official data on the corresponding chronological dynamics of the debt-GDP ratio.

In terms of state debt, especially external debt, the choice of the research period was largely determined by the trend of increasing debt volumes.

Until 2008, the state debt of the Republic of Armenia periodically registered a decreasing trend, but due to the global financial and economic crisis of 2009, the growth of the debt-GDP ratio amounted to 24.2%. Moreover, the depreciation

---

[112] See the same place.

of the national currency against foreign currency by 23.2 percentage points was a factor significantly contributing to the growth.

The next sharp rise in the debt-GDP ratio was recorded in 2016, due to economic sanctions imposed against Russia, which is the main trading partner of the Republic of Armenia. As a result, the RA public debt index recorded an increase of about 8%.[113]

2020 began with the coronavirus crisis and ended with the Second Artsakh War, causing both financial and human losses. An extremely difficult economic and political situation was created for the Republic of Armenia. Due to military operations, the volume of military expenditures, which are a spending priority, increased by about 40 billion drams in 2020. Restrictions due to the pandemic reduced tax revenues by about 113 billion drams.[114]

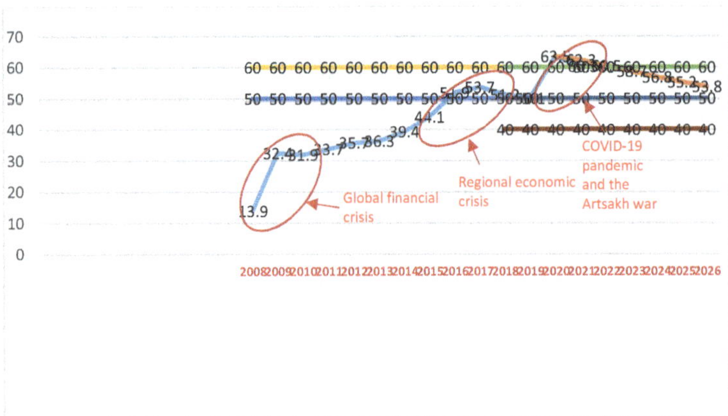

Source: Ministry of Finance and Statistical Committee of the Republic of Armenia.

Figure 8. Dynamics of the RA government debt in 2000-2021[115]

---

[113] "Revised Program for Reducing the Debt Burden of the RA Government for 2022-2026", p. 4, available at the following link: https://www.e-gov.am/u_files/file/decrees/kar/GV73-6817-ACFF-CBF2/1010.2.pdf

[114] GRIGORYAN, A.(2021). "PROBLEMS OF DEBT SECURITY OF THE RA ECONOMY IN THE CONTEXT OF THE ARTSAKH WAR", SCIENTIFIC ARTSAKH № 1(8), 2021, DOI: 10.52063/25792652-2021.1-181 pp. 181-187, available at the following link: https://arar.sci.am/dlibra/publication/293297/edition/269281

[115] "Revised Program for Reducing the Debt Burden of the RA Government for 2022-2026", p. 4, available at the following link: https://www.e-gov.am/u_files/file/decrees/kar/GV73-6817-ACFF-CBF2/1010.2.pdf

According to data published by the World Bank, in 2020, Armenia was one of the leaders in the volume of economic decline among Eastern European and CIS countries. In 2020, the economic situation was worse than in Armenia only in Montenegro, Croatia, Kosovo and Kyrgyzstan. As for Armenia's immediate neighbors, according to the World Bank, last year the economic decline in Georgia was 6 percent, and in Azerbaijan 5 percent. Thus, the state debt/GDP ratio was 66.5% as of the end of 2020, and is forecast to be 67% as of the end of 2021. The RA Law "On State Debt" stipulates that the limit threshold for the ratio of government debt to gross domestic product of the Republic of Armenia as of December 31 of each year is 60 percent.[116] Government debt should not have exceeded 60% of GDP. However, as of December 31, 2020, the specified threshold was exceeded, however, it will not be considered a violation of the provisions of the law, since the same law also establishes exceptions under which it is allowed to exceed this threshold. War, the situation caused by the pandemic are among the exceptions.[117]

In 2021, the RA Government's debt-to-GDP ratio exceeded the 60% threshold set by RA legislation, amounting to 66.5%. According to the RA Government's 2022-2026 Debt Reduction Program, the RA Government's debt should be reduced below 60% of GDP within 5 years, due to which, with the revision of the Program, forecasts are presented with a 4-year horizon.[118]

A significant increase in government debt was observed in 2016. Compared to 2015, an increase of 7.8 percentage points was recorded. Moreover, the depreciation behavior of the national exchange rate against foreign currencies is common in the observed crisis periods. In 2021, the Armenian dram depreciated, mainly due to the developments in the first half of the year as a result of expectations and uncertainties formed as a result of the pandemic and the Artsakh war. The Armenian dram depreciated against the US dollar, the Euro, and the Russian ruble in 2021 by 2.9%, 6.4%, and 0.6%, respectively.

---

[116] "Law of the Republic of Armenia on State Debt", Article 5, available at the following link: https://www.arlis.am/documentview.aspx?docid=119085

[117] "Armenia's public debt is serviced without obstacles during the war", available at the following link: https://minfin.am/hy/content/hayastani_petakan_partqy_paterazmi_orerin_spasarkvum_e_aranc_khochyndotneri/

[118] «Revised programs for 2023-2025 state medium-term expenditures and 2022-2026 reduction of the RA government debt burden", p. 7, available at the following link: https://minfin.am/hy/page/petakan_mijnazhamket_tsakhseri_tsragre/

Due to the above factors, after some depreciation in the first half of 2021, the Armenian dram began to appreciate against the US dollar, mainly due to the improvement in the balance of goods and services and a significant inflow of remittances. In 2021, the maximum fluctuation of the dram against the US dollar was 11.6%, the maximum exchange rate of 537.4 was recorded on April 8, and the average exchange rate for the year was 503.8. In contrast to the depreciation of the annual average exchange rate, in December 2021, compared to December of the previous year, the Armenian dram appreciated against the US dollar by about 7%. The average exchange rate of the Armenian dram against the Russian ruble in 2021 compared to the previous year depreciated by 0.6%, due to the strengthening of the position of the Russian ruble in the international market, and in December, compared to December of the previous year, it showed an appreciation trend of 6.4%.[119]

The decrease in the government debt/GDP ratio in 2021 was mainly due to the appreciation of the Armenian dram and real GDP growth, while the fiscal policy stance continued to be a factor contributing to the increase in the debt burden. The decrease in the government debt/GDP ratio by 3.2 percentage points was contributed by the appreciation of the Armenian dram against the US dollar by -4.6 percentage points, economic growth by -3.2 percentage points, and the decrease in the real interest rate by 2.7 percentage points (due to the decrease in the nominal interest rate and the acceleration of inflation).[120]

In general, the trend of debt growth was predictable due to the negative realities known to us. However, the sharp increase in external debt carries certain risks, the materialization of which will undermine the tools for the smooth implementation of fiscal and budgetary rules.

From this perspective, although there is still no general approach among researchers and thinkers of different periods on effective debt management, there is always talk about the ability to further service the external borrowing involved, emphasizing the attraction of loans on more favorable terms.

---

[119] "MACROECONOMIC AND FISCAL DEVELOPMENTS OF THE REPUBLIC OF ARMENIA IN 2021" pp. 13-14, available at the following link: https://www.minfin.am/website/images/files/%20%20%202021%20%20%20%20%20%20.docx

[120] See the same place page 19.

During the period under review, due to the reduction in the volume of exports of the Republic of Armenia, as well as the already mentioned negative challenges, we have emphasized the study of the correlation between government debt and economic growth in the Republic of Armenia and the member states of the Eurasian Economic Union (hereinafter referred to as the EAEU).

The indicators of economic growth and government debt growth in the EAEU countries indicate that there is a trend of economic decline in the member states of the economic union, as well as an increase in debt obligations. Although the International Monetary Fund predicted “modest” economic growth in Armenia in 2021, a more than 7 percent decline in GDP was observed in Armenia in 2021.

The Eurasian Economic Union is already a well-known reality, the creation of which reflects the state interests of the member states of the Union. It should be noted that the EAEU is an economic union, which primarily means the creation of a single economic region. In order to create such a single economic region, both the governments of the member states of the Union and the Board of the Eurasian Economic Commission have taken the necessary measures and effective work, adopting relevant laws and other regulatory legal documents for harmonization, despite the significant differences between the countries.[121]

In this section of the book, we have addressed the logical interrelationship between the debt and economic growth of member states of an economic union.

Russia: In 2018, the Russian economy grew by 2.3%, the highest rate since 2012. In the medium term, GDP growth is expected to range between 1.4% and 2.2%. Since the beginning of 2019, the Russian economy has shown signs of slowing down. In the first quarter of 2019, GDP growth was 0.8%. The slowdown in consumer activity, coupled with the increase in the VAT rate and the decline in real incomes, constrained economic growth in early 2019, along with a temporary acceleration in inflation.

In 2019, the decline in consumer activity and the restrictions on access to international financial markets for the banking and corporate sectors are factors

[121] Melkumyan, M. (2015). "Problems of Economic Development of the Republic of Armenia within the Framework of the EAEU"; Proceedings of the 25th ASUE Conference "KNOWLEDGE, INNOVATION AND DEVELOPMENT", Yerevan: Economist, 2015, p. 251, available at the following link: https://asue.am/upload/files/II_Baj._tarmacvac.pdf

that negatively affect economic dynamics. Thus, GDP growth in 2019 was expected to be 1.4%, in 2020 - 2.1%, in 2021 - 2.2%.

A gradual stabilization of the growth rate of public debt was expected, but it will remain above 50% (set by the EAEU Treaty) over the forecast horizon, the need for which may arise when implementing joint measures. At the same time, the general government deficit will be below 3% of GDP.

Belarus: Favorable external conditions and expansionary policies had a positive impact on economic growth in 2018, however, the economy gradually slowed down towards the end of the year due to the decrease in the stimulating effect of monetary policy, the increase in oil imports and the economic slowdown in trading partner countries. In 2018, the economic growth rate increased to 3%, which was the best indicator since 2011. However, it should be noted that structural constraints and economic Vulnerabilities are hindering potential GDP growth rates. Economic growth will be limited to 1.5-2.0% in the medium term.

Kazakhstan: Acceleration of inflationary processes against the background of stimulating economic growth and maintaining a favorable external environment has become the main trend until mid-2020. The decline in investment efficiency will negatively affect the potential GDP growth rates. Despite the fiscal and monetary policy stimuli, the growth rate over the forecast horizon will be lower than that achieved in 2017-2018, which indicates the need to change the structure of the economy to improve the quality of investments.

The forecast for GDP growth in 2019 was 3.4%. In 2019-2021 Over the forecast horizon, the weakening of the expansionary fiscal policy and the overall decline in the efficiency of public investment will affect the decline in growth rates, which will also affect the long-term GDP growth rate, which will amount to 2.9% by the end of 2023.

Kyrgyzstan: The increase in growth rates in the first quarter of 2019 was due to a 1.5-fold increase in gold production at the Kumtor mine (compared to the same period in 2018), which, among other things, allowed to improve the foreign trade balance. However, the low efficiency of the interest rate wave does not provide the expected stimulating effect for the economy. In the first quarter of 2020, the state budget was executed with a surplus of 2.5% of GDP, which is associated with uneven budget execution during the year. In the medium term, the budget will remain socially oriented. Gradual fiscal consolidation will help to improve fiscal policy and debt sustainability. At the same time, the significant level of dependence on external financing and the high costs of raising funds in the domestic market are sources of great risks for the economy.[122]

Republic of Armenia. In 2018, Armenia's GDP growth rate remained the highest among the EAEU member states, however, it slowed down to 5.2% compared to 7.5% in the previous year. Ongoing structural reforms and expansionary monetary policy provide the necessary support to the economy against the backdrop of the slowdown observed in the main trading partner countries.

The significant impact of disruptions in the main partner channels of trade turnover with our republic, especially at the initial stage, due to the Russian-Ukrainian conflict, was significant in economic terms due to the restriction of Russian markets. Moreover, in the initial days, uncertainty was noticeable in the Republic of Armenia due to disruptions in the main partner directions of the Russian Federation, as well as the "sanctions" still in force against the Russian Federation create difficulties in the implementation of bank transfers. As for communication with the Ukrainian markets, we can note that the economic impact of the Republic of Armenia is assessed as small.

[122] Eurasian Economic Commission Forecast prepared in April-May 2019. Forecast data cutoff date is 15 April 2019. EAEU Member States Main Economic Indicators 2019-2021 Forecast pp. 5-13, available at the following link:
http://www.eurasiancommission.org/en/act/integr_i_makroec/dep_makroec_pol/economyPrognoz/Documents/EAEU%20Member%20States%20Forecast_fin.pdf

Table 2.

Expected indicators of economic growth and government debt growth in the EEU countries[123]

Country	Government debt, % of GDP Economic growth, % Government debt/GDP growth				Government debt, % of GDP Economic growth, % Government debt/GDP growth			Government debt, % of GDP Economic growth, % Government debt/GDP growth	
	2019 Fact	2020 Fact	2021 Fact	2022 Fact	2020 Fact	2021 Fact	2022 Forecast	2020: compared to 2019, %	2020թ.` compared to 2021, %
Armenia	49.9	63.5	60.3	58.4	-7.3	5.7	10.8	13.6	-3.2
Russia	13.9	19.2	16.99	16.19	-4.1	-3.7	-3.5	5.3	-2.21
Belarus	41.9	47.49	41.18	34.98	-3.0	-0.4	-6.2	5.59	-6.31
Kazakhstan	19.9	26.36	25.1	23.28	-2.7	1.26	3	6.46	-1.26
Kyrgyzstan	54.1	68.1	61.12	50.9	-12.0	3.6	5.5	14	-6.98

Data: www.statista.com

[123] IMF (2020). "World Economic Outlook Database", available at the following link: https://www.imf.org/en/Publications/SPROLLs/world-economic-outlook-databases#sort=%40imfdate%20descending

Thus, it can be concluded that in the Republic of Armenia and other EAEU partner countries, in 2020, compared to 2019, a sharp increase in debt was recorded due to anti-crisis measures aimed at mitigating the negative economic consequences of the COVID-19 pandemic, which, however, were not sufficient to avoid an economic recession. As a result, the expected growth rate of debt in the Republic of Armenia and other EAEU partner countries, according to IMF forecasts, will continue to be at an average level.

Thus, although the increase in the volume of public debt in 2020 had objective reasons for justification, due to the pandemic and the Artsakh war, nevertheless, the absence of necessary measures from the point of view of public debt sustainability may lead to fiscal "imbalances" in the long term. On the one hand, planned capital expenditures in 2020 were not implemented, leading to a decline in economic efficiency, the indicator of which in December 2020 touched almost 8%, on the other hand, current expenditures for the following year have continuously increased. In the coming years, it is necessary for the RA government to review its spending policy, setting spending priorities, conditioned by the implementation of effective steps to overcome the consequences of the Second Artsakh War, as well as the situation caused by the pandemic. At the same time, it is necessary to identify and reduce financial resources directed to all types of ineffective programs, injecting them primarily into the implementation of programs that create economic growth. In this way, it is also possible to increase the potential for ensuring economic growth in the medium term.

We consider it necessary to note that in 2020, the RA, being in a war period, nevertheless continued to service its external public debt on time and in full, in particular, on September 30, 2020, it fully repaid the balance of the $700 million debt received in 2013, about $97.7 million. At the same time, the RA issued Eurobonds worth $500 million, but with a lower yield of 4.2%, which means that the burden of this debt for Armenia will be lower than the previous one. The new Eurobonds were issued for a period of 10 years, which Armenia is obliged to repay in 2025 and 2029. That is, in the coming years, Armenia will also have to allocate more money to servicing interest on external debt than to inject financial resources into the development of such sectors as education, culture, healthcare.

The highest economic growth rates in the region in 2022 were recorded in Armenia and Georgia. This is also the picture of the regional picture of economic growth forecasts in the World Bank's 2023 "Global Economic Prospects" report (see table 3).[124]

Table 3.

World Bank economic growth projections for the region[125]

Countries Economic growth forecasts by year, %	Countries Economic growth forecasts by year, %		
	2022թ.	**2023թ.**	**2024թ.**
Armenia	10.8	4.1	4.8
Georgia	10	4	5
Iran	2.9	2.2	1.9
Azerbaijan	4.2	2.8	2.6
Russia	-3.5	-3.3	1.6
Belarus	-6.2	-2.3	2.5
Kazakhstan	3	3.5	4
Kyrgyzstan	5.5	3.5	4

Against the backdrop of the forecasts, it is noteworthy that the report predicts a slowdown in global economic growth rates, amounting to about 1.7% in 2023. However, according to the World Bank forecasts, the economic growth rates of Armenia in 2023 and 2024 will also be considered the highest in the region. In particular, according to the report, the economic growth of Armenia in 2023 will be 4.1%, and in 2024 - 4.8%. In general, the economic growth rates of Armenia continue to be assessed as the highest in the region in the forecast years. At the end of 2022, the state debt of Armenia in dram terms amounted to 4,479.5 billion drams, an increase of 4.9 percent compared to the previous year.[126] At the end of the year, the Armenian Government's debt in dram terms amounted to

[124] World Bank Group (2023). “Global Economic Prospects”, available at the following link: https://openknowledge.worldbank.org/bitstream/handle/10986/38030/GEP-January-2023.pdf?fbclid=IwAR3Vfu4dbas5MvoHn_dWlvB0dKwds3OeNHXWEIs44IL_EuMs8Uztb nX9h08

[125] Data from the World Bank.

[126] Dynamics of summary data on the debt of the RA government for 2013-2022, available at the following link:
https://www.minfin.am/hy/page/petakan_partqi_veraberyal_ampop_tvyalner/

4,252.5 billion drams, an increase of 4.2% compared to the same period last year.[127]

In 2022, the external debt indicator of the Central Bank of the Republic of Armenia also increased somewhat, amounting to 227.0 billion drams at the end of the year. During the observed period, an upward trend was observed in both domestic and external debt indicators. In particular, at the end of 2021, the domestic public debt of the Republic of Armenia in dram terms amounted to 1,237.4 billion drams, in 2022 - 1,267.8 billion drams, the external public debt amounted to 3,192.2 billion drams in 2021, and in 2022 - 3,211.7 billion drams, respectively. In general, although the public debt of the Republic of Armenia has increased, the Government of the Republic of Armenia has managed to reduce the Debt-GDP ratio to 47 percent by the end of 2022 as a result of fiscal consolidation, while the program forecast for 2021 predicted that the indicator would be reduced to a level below 60 percent. The 47 percent indicator recorded at the end of 2022 can be considered the result of the flexible policy pursued by the RA Government, the improvement of the quality of debt management, and, of course, the impact of external factors, which is a very important signal from the point of view of financial reliability.

In 2023, due to double-digit economic growth, the average income of the RA increased, as a result of which the possibility of obtaining external borrowed funds on preferential terms was reduced, that is, if necessary, the RA will already obtain external loans on market terms.

According to the official data of the RA Statistical Committee, the structure of the RA public debt underwent significant changes in 2022. For comparison, we can note that if the share of external debt in the structure of the RA public debt in 2021 was 70.6 percent, then in 2022 the share of external debt decreased, making up 63.4 percent. In this context, we emphasize that during the period under review,

[127] Matevosyan A., Grigoryan A., (2023). "THE APPROACH TO ASSESSING THE IMPACT OF ECONOMIC ACTIVITY GROWTH AND FOREIGN EXCHANGE DEBT OF THE RA" INTERNATIONAL SCIENTIFIC AND EDUCATIONAL CENTER OF THE RA "PROBLEMS OF COMPETITIVE EDUCATION AND SCIENCE IN A RAPIDLY CHANGING WORLD" PROCEEDINGS OF THE INTERNATIONAL SCIENTIFIC CONFERENCE JUNE 21, 2023, ISSN 2579-2903, pp. 327-347, https://www.isec.am/images/gitakan_hraparakumner/Gitajoxov_2023.pdf

the share of domestic debt in the structure of public debt increased, reaching 29.4 percent in 2021 and 36.6 percent in 2022.

Although certain risks have arisen in terms of the manageability of external public debt, we believe that the 2022 debt-to-GDP ratio was a consequence not only of the influence of external factors, but also of a quality state policy.

Thus, taking into account the fact that the attraction of external credit funds contains foreign exchange risk, we believe that the development of the domestic public debt market will mitigate the currency risk as much as possible, which is tangible from the point of view of assessing the risks of external public debt.

In the context of reducing external public debt and implementing a quality debt policy in general, the Government's ability to provide debt service allocations is of key importance, as well as loans attracted in foreign currency, which contain the risk of exchange rate fluctuations, since the more funds are allocated to debt service, the fewer funds will be generated for capital-generating areas. It is also noteworthy that in the event of unfavorable foreign exchange fluctuations, external debt servicing costs may increase, increasing the demand for financial resources to be used for debt servicing.

However, certain risks have arisen in terms of external debt manageability. The debt-to-GDP ratio recorded at the beginning of the year was significantly supported by the appreciation of the national currency. Although external public debt servicing has “become more expensive” compared to the previous year, the appreciation of the dram has significantly compensated for the debt servicing risk.

In 2022, the RA state budget deficit was largely financed at the expense of domestic borrowings, by 79.2% or 252.0 billion drams, while financing at the expense of external sources amounted to 20.8% or 66.2 billion drams. According to the draft state budget of the Republic of Armenia, the deficit for 2023 was planned at 3.1 percent of GDP. In the case of a projected 7 percent economic growth, the Government's goal of setting the state budget deficit within 2.5-3.0% of GDP is an optimistic approach, which will allow reducing the Debt-GDP ratio. The share of external public debt in the structure of the RA state debt in 2023 is forecast at 58.6 percent. At the end of 2022, this indicator was 63.4%. For comparison, in 2018 the indicator was 78%.

The indicators of recent years show that the specific weight of external public debt in the structure of the RA public debt has lost its position due to the growth of domestic debt volumes. In addition to being part of the RA Government's public debt management strategy, this trend also has a favorable impact in terms of reducing exchange rate risks. Of the 180.8 billion drams of interest payments paid on the RA Government's debt in 2021, 60% or 108.3 billion drams were domestic interest payments, while interest payments paid on external debt amounted to 40% or 72.5 billion drams.

In 2022, the majority of interest payments paid on the RA Government's debt from the RA state budget were directed to servicing the domestic debt - 63.5% or 125.9 billion drams, and to servicing external debt - 36.5% or 72.4 billion drams, of which the servicing of interest payments on loans received from external sources amounted to 17.7 percent or 35.0 billion drams. Debt service costs in 2023 are planned at 272 billion drams, i.e. 10.5% of budgeted expenditures or 2.9% of GDP. The increase in interest payments this year is planned at 0.3 percentage points of GDP.

According to forecasts, the weighted average interest rate on the RA debt service in 2023 is projected at 6.4 percent, an increase of 1.2 percentage points compared to the previous year. Moreover, the interest rate on external debt is projected at 4.1 percent. Naturally, the increase in interest rates is due to a number of factors, the key of which is the increase in interest rates in international financial markets, which also has an impact on the RA financial market.

The increase in the cost of servicing the Republic of Armenia's external debt is also a response to the debt involved with a floating interest rate. In the structure of the Republic of Armenia, liabilities assumed with a floating interest rate make up about 18 percent, therefore, an unfavorable change in the interest rate increases the cost of servicing the assumed liability.

In the structure of the Republic of Armenia's external debt, there are loans involved in foreign currency, the service rates of which increase in line with GDP growth. According to forecasts, in 2023 the specific weight of the latter in the debt structure will make up about 3.6 percent, while in 2022 it was 2 percent.

The service of the Republic of Armenia's debt has also become more expensive due to the increase in dram debt in the structure of the state debt, since in the Republic of Armenia, in contrast to the 4.1 percent weighted average interest rate on external debt, the interest rate on domestic debt is 10.9 percent.

Thus, we can record that the 46.7 percent Debt-to-GDP ratio recorded in 2022 as a result of fiscal consolidation by the Government of the Republic of Armenia was the lowest indicator compared to the previous 5 years, which will provide the Republic of Armenia with a guarantee of higher reliability and creditworthiness in the context of deepening the integration of financial markets.[128]

In summary, we note that, having studied the dynamics of the RA external public debt during the war and "Covid" periods, we can state that although the external public debt was serviced without obstacles, we believe that in order to ensure the manageability of the RA public debt, debt management should be based not on the issue of reducing the size or continuous growth of the debt, but on the goal of increasing the efficiency of its use, which will contribute to economic growth, neutralizing the risks of servicing and repaying the public debt as much as possible. In other words, the foreign debt funds received should be generated in the form of investments in sectors that are considered the most promising and that promise real economic growth. In this way, it will also be possible to avoid inheriting the problematic debt burden to future generations.[129]

---

[128] MATEVOSYAN A., GRIGHORYAN A., (2023). "THE APPROACH TO ASSESSING THE IMPACT OF ECONOMIC ACTIVITY GROWTH AND FOREIGN EXCHANGE DEBT OF THE RA" INTERNATIONAL SCIENTIFIC AND EDUCATIONAL CENTER OF THE RA "PROBLEMS OF COMPETITIVE EDUCATION AND SCIENCE IN A RAPIDLY CHANGING WORLD" PROCEEDINGS OF THE INTERNATIONAL SCIENTIFIC CONFERENCE JUNE 21, 2023, ISSN 2579-2903, pp. 327-347, https://www.isec.am/images/gitakan_hraparakumner/Gitajoxov_2023.pdf

[129] GRIGORYAN, A. (2021). "PROBLEMS OF DEBT SECURITY OF THE RA ECONOMY IN THE CONTEXT OF THE ARTSAKH WAR", SCIENTIFIC ARTSAKH № 1(8), 2021, DOI: 10.52063/25792652-2021.1-181 p. 187, available at the following link: https://arar.sci.am/dlibra/publication/293297/edition/269281

CHAPTER 3. WAYS TO IMPROVE THE EFFICIENCY OF FOREIGN STATE DEBT MANAGEMENT. STUDIES FROM ARMENIA

3.1 Problems and solutions of state debt management in the context of structural peculiarities.

It is no secret that the financial market is the most sensitive environment to expectations, especially the state bond market. One of the possible sources of servicing and repaying the state debt of the RA is the income received from bonds. For this purpose, the RA issues state bonds in the local capital market, while at the same time successfully participating in the international capital market. The placement volumes indicate that the RA state bonds, although they provide low profitability in the long term, are nevertheless considered an attractive and reliable investment instrument from the point of view of investors, since they contain minimal risk.

Within the framework of the study of the prospects for the development of the bond market, we assessed the relationship between government bonds and a number of factors. The primary factor was considered to be real wages, being the main source of savings formation. Thus, we assessed the relationship between real wages and the volume of transactions with government bonds using the correlation coefficient. The Pearson correlation coefficient shows the linear relationship between the two variables and is in the range [-1;1] (the closer it is to 1, the stronger the correlation and vice versa).

The purpose of this section of the book is to substantiate the realism of the proposed new approach to improving management due to the structure of the RA public debt, during the implementation of which the task was set to study the structural features of the RA public debt in recent years.

As a result, the need to deepen the development of the domestic public debt market in order to weaken the specific weight of external debt in the structure of the public debt was substantiated through methodological analysis, since the RA public debt is considered sensitive to exchange rate "shocks". For this purpose, estimates of the correlation between real wages and government debt were made based on the Pearson correlation coefficient (r) and Spearman's rank correlation coefficient (rs). The results of the estimates indicate a positive relationship.

In international practice, there are various debt attraction tools. The most commonly used is debt attraction from financial and credit organizations, as well as from individuals and legal entities.

In the structure of the RA state debt, an increase in the specific weight of domestic state debt has been observed over the past ten years, due to the volume of transactions concluded with state bonds. The picture is particularly important from the point of view of assessing the stability of the state debt, which, although stable in recent years, is sensitive to interest rate and refinancing risks.

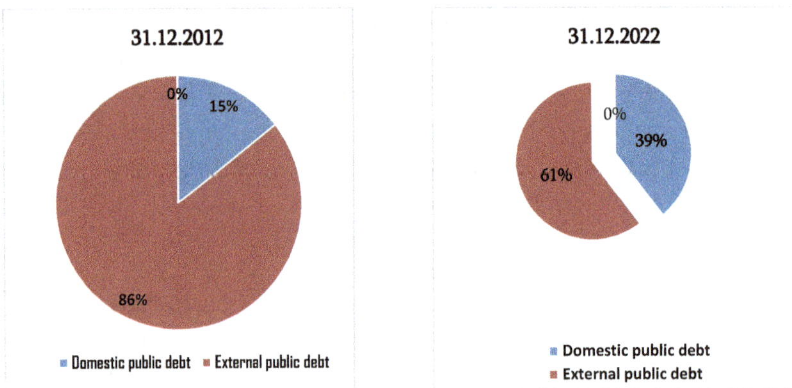

Figure 9. Weights of domestic and external public debt in the structure of the RA public debt in 2012-2022

Table 4.

Calculation of the correlation assessment of real wages and government bonds in 2009-2021[130]

X – Mx	Y – My	(X - Mx)^2	(Y - My)^2	(X - Mx) (Y - My)
4.354 1.354 - 0.246 - 0.846 - 1.446 2.654 2.654 - 3.946 - 3.646 - 1.546 0.254 - 1.646 2.054 Mx: 105.546	102401.231 -20665.769 -16960.769 -12981.769 -37964.769 251925.231 -37964.769 -37964.769 -37964.769 -37964.769 -37964.769 -37964.769 -37964.769 My: 37964.769	18.956 1.833 0.061 0.716 2.091 7.043 7.043 15.572 13.294 2.391 0.064 2.710 4.218 Sum: 75.992	10486012063.053 427074017.899 287667692.899 168526332.361 1441323702.746 63466321898.130 1441323702.746 1441323702.746 1441323702.746 1441323702.746 1441323702.746 1441323702.746 1441323702.746 Sum: 86366191626.308	445839.205 -27978.272 4174.959 10984.574 54902.897 668570.805 - 100752.657 149814.820 138425.389 58699.374 -9637.211 62495.851 -77973.795 Sum: 1377565.938

Result in Details & Calculation	Key
X Values ∑ = 1372.1 Mean = 105.546 ∑(X - Mx)2 = SSx = 75.992 Y Values ∑ = 493542 Mean = 37964.769 ∑(Y - My)2 = SSy = 86366191626.308 X and Y Combined N = 13 ∑(X - Mx)(Y - My) = 1377565.938 R Calculation r = ∑((X - My)(Y - Mx)) / √((SSx)(SSy)) r = 1377565.938 / √((75.992)(86366191626.308)) = 0.5377 Meta Numerics (cross-check) r = 0.5377	X: X Values Y: Y Values Mx: Mean of X Values My: Mean of Y Values X - Mx & Y - My: Deviation scores (X - Mx)2 & (Y - My)2: Deviation Squared (X - Mx) (Y - My): Product of Deviation Scores

[130] Calculations by the author.

Thus, within the framework of studying the development of the bond market, assessing the relationship between government bonds and real wages, we can highlight the factor of increasing real wages as the main source of savings formation as a key factor in weakening the dependence on external debt.

Table 5.

Real wage and government bond indices for 2009-2021

Real wage, index (%) [131]	Government bond[132]
109.9	140366
106.9	17299
105.3	21004
104.7	24983
104.1	274 175
108.2	289890
108.2	289 034
101.6	508 333
101.9	549 730
104	560 739
105.8	681 050
103.9	958 834
107.6	1 208 887

As a result of the correlation assessment of the relationship between real wages and government bonds, the R value is 0.5377, meaning that there is a moderate positive correlation between the variables.

Based on the positive relationship between real wages and government bonds, we considered it necessary to also conduct an assessment of the above variables using the Spearman rank correlation coefficient. The results of the assessment are presented below.

[131] Data: RA Statistical Committee www.armstat.am

[132] Data: RA Ministry of Finance www.minfin.am

Table 6.

Assessment of the relationship between real wages and government bonds using the Spearman rank correlation coefficient[133]

Spearman's rank correlation coefficient (rs)[134] **Results** $r_s = 0.5285$	
Parameter	Value
Spearman's rank correlation coefficient (rs)	0.5285
P-value	0.06333
Covariance	88833.7193
Sample size (n)	13
Statistic	2.0649

According to the Spearman rank correlation coefficient, if the result is -1, the correlation is considered negative, if it is close to 0, there is no linear correlation, and if the result is almost close to 1, the correlation is considered positive.

The results of the Spearman rank correlation coefficient assessment of the relationship between the real wage of the Republic of Armenia and government bonds allow us to confirm that the relationship between the variables X and Y is assessed as positive.

We checked the results of the Spearman rank correlation assessment using the test published by Samuel Sanford Shapiro and Martin Wilk, the Shapiro-Wilk Test (α=0.05). As a result of the test calculation, we can record that the distribution of the residuals follows a normal distribution.

In order to substantiate the realism of the proposed approach, we also conducted a correlation assessment in this subsection of the study for the period 2013 - 2022. Between the average monthly salary in the Republic of Armenia and the volume of government bonds placed.

---

[133] Calculations by the author.

[134] Calculations by the author.

Table 7.

Calculation of the correlation coefficient between the average monthly salary in the Republic of Armenia and the volume of government bonds placed 2013 – 2022

Years	Average monthly salary in Armenia, million drams, x	Volume of government bonds, million drams, y	X_i^2	X_iY_i	Y_i^2
2013	0,146	103,5	0,021	15,1	10712,3
2014	0,159	104,1	0,025	16,6	10836,8
2015	0,171	103	0,029	17,6	10609,0
2016	0,174	100,7	0,030	17,5	10140,5
2017	0,178	107,7	0,032	19,2	11599,3
2018	0,173	105,6	0,030	18,3	11151,4
2019	0,183	107,8	0,033	19,7	11620,8
2020	0,189	92,5	0,036	17,5	8556,3
2021	0,204	105,8	0,042	21,6	11193,6
2022	0,236	114,2	0,056	27,0	13041,6
Total	1,813	1044,9	0,334	190,0	109461,6
Average score					

Calculations by the author.

$$r_{xy} = \frac{\overline{XY} - \overline{X}\overline{Y}}{\sigma_x \sigma_y}$$

$$\sigma_x = \sqrt{\overline{X^2} - (\overline{X})^2}$$

$$\sigma_y = \sqrt{\overline{Y^2} - (\overline{Y})^2}$$

$$\sigma_x = \sqrt{0,033 - 0,032} = 0,032$$

$$\sigma_y = \sqrt{10946,2 - 10920,3} = 5,09$$

$$r_{xy} = \frac{19-18,9}{5,09 \; x \; 0,032} = 0,625$$

As a result of the assessment, since we obtained a correlation coefficient of 0.65, we can state that the relationship between the average monthly salary of the Republic of Armenia and the volume of government bonds placed is noticeable.

Considering the positive relationship between the selected variables, we conducted a regression analysis between the average monthly salary of the Republic of Armenia and the indicators of the external public debt of the Republic of Armenia for 2013-2022.

$$\begin{cases} na_0 + a_1 \sum x = \sum y \\ a_0 \sum x + a_1 \sum x^2 = \sum xy \end{cases}$$

$$\begin{cases} \mathbf{10}a_0 + \mathbf{1,8}a_1 = \mathbf{22458,2} \\ \mathbf{1,8}a_0 + \mathbf{0,334}a_1 = \mathbf{4146,6} \end{cases}$$

$$\begin{cases} \mathbf{10}a_0 + \mathbf{1,8}a_1 = \mathbf{22458,2} \\ \mathbf{1,08}a_0 + \mathbf{1,8}a_1 = \mathbf{2486,9} \end{cases}$$

$$\mathbf{8,92}a_0 = 19971{,}3$$

$$a_0 = 2238{,}9$$

$$\mathbf{22389} + \mathbf{1,8}a_1 = \mathbf{22458,2}$$

$$a_1 = 38{,}4$$

Therefore, the univariate regression model will be:

$$\hat{Y}_x = \mathbf{2238,9} + \mathbf{38,4}x$$

Table 8.

Regression calculation of the average monthly salary of the Republic of Armenia and the external public debt of the Republic of Armenia for 2013-2022.

Year	Average monthly salary in Armenia, million drams, x	RA external public debt, million drams, y	X_i^2	X_iY_i	$\hat{Y}_x = a_0 + a_1x$
2013	0,146	1375,4	0,021	200,8	2244,5
2014	0,159	1592,0	0,025	253,1	2245,0
2015	0,171	1862,0	0,029	318,4	2245,5
2016	0,174	2080,3	0,030	362,0	2245,6
2017	0,178	2378,1	0,032	423,3	2245,7
2018	0,173	2412,0	0,030	417,3	2245,5
2019	0,183	2540,1	0,033	464,8	2245,9
2020	0,189	2926,2	0,036	553,1	2246,2
2021	0,204	2972,4	0,042	606,4	2246,7
2022	0,236	2319,7	0,056	547,4	2248,0
Total	**1,8**	**22458,2**	**0,334**	**4146,6**	**22458,6**

Calculations by the author.

As a result, the change in the average monthly salary of the Republic of Armenia will lead to a change in the state debt of the Republic of Armenia by -0.24%. In general, such an assessment result was predictable, taking into account the current level of salaries. In this context, based on the assessment results, we also conducted a regression assessment between the indicators of external state debt recorded in 2013-2022 and the state budget revenues, official transfers, and the gross domestic product of the Republic of Armenia, which were considered as primary impact variables.

$$\begin{cases} na_0 + a_1 \sum X_1 + a_2 \sum X_2 = \sum Y \\ a_0 \sum X_1 + a_1 \sum X_1^2 + a_2 \sum X_1 X_2 = \sum X_1 Y \\ a_0 \sum X_2 + a_1 \sum X_1 X_2 + a_2 \sum X_2^2 = \sum X_2 Y \end{cases}$$

$$\begin{cases} 10a_0 + 14007558,9a_1 + 59281684,5a_2 = 22458,2 \\ 14007558,9a_0 + 20503852759695,3a_1 + 86372429987436,5a_2 = 32420488243,7 \\ 59281684,5a_0 + 86372429987436,5a_1 + 364341448801996,0a_2 = 136808052477,4 \end{cases}$$

$$a_0 = 641{,}6$$

$$a_1 = 0{,}0006$$

$$a_2 = 0{,}0001$$

Therefore, the multivariate regression model will be:

$$\hat{Y}_x = 641,6 - 0,0006X_1 + 0,0001X_2$$

Table 9.

Multiple regression calculation of the RA state budget revenues, official transfers, RA gross domestic product and RA external public debt for 2013 - 2022.

Year	RA State Budget Revenues and Official Transfers, at Current Prices, Million AMD, X_1	Armenia's GDP, at market prices, million drams, X_2	Armenia's external public debt, million drams, Y	X_1^2	X_1X_2	X_1Y	X_2^2	X_2Y	$\hat{Y}_x$
2013	1071370,6	4555638,2	1375,4	1147834962544,4	4880776831716,9	1473563123,2	20753839409299,2	6265824780,3	1740,0
2014	1144762,7	4828626,3	1592,0	1310481639311,3	5527631280479,0	1822462218,4	23315631945051,7	7687173069,6	1811,3
2015	1167744	5043633,2	1862,0	1363626049536,0	5889672407500,8	2174339328,0	25438235856142,2	9391245018,4	1846,6
2016	1171107,3	5067293,5	2080,3	1371492308113,3	5934344409092,6	2436254516,2	25677463415142,2	10541490668,1	1851,0
2017	1237780,8	5564493,3	2378,1	1532101308848,6	6887622968468,6	2943566520,5	30963585685744,9	13232921516,7	1940,7
2018	1341690,6	6017035,2	2412,0	1800133666128,4	8072999567709,1	3236157727,2	36204712598039,0	14513088902,4	2048,3
2019	1565488,9	6543321,8	2540,1	2450755496023,2	10243497647028,0	3976498354,9	42815060178355,2	16620691704,2	2235,2

2020	1560655,3	6181902,6	2926,2	2435644965418,1	9647819056773,8	4566789538,9	38215919755886,8	18089483388,1	2196,2
2021	1683831,5	6982962,5	2972,4	2835288520392,3	11758132220818,7	5005020750,6	48761765276406,2	20756157735,0	2350,2
2022	2063127,2	8496777,9	2319,7	4256493843379,8	17529933597848,9	4785836165,8	72195234681928,4	19709975694,6	2729,2
Total	14007558,9	59281684,5	22458,2	20503852759695,3	86372429987436,5	32420488243,7	364341448801996,0	136808052477,4	20748,7

Calculations by the author.

Thus, the calculations show that the change in the revenues of the state budget of the Republic of Armenia and the gross domestic product will lead to a change in the external public debt of the Republic of Armenia of 0.0006 and 0.0001 million drams, respectively.

In summary, we note that the coefficient estimates used allow us to substantiate that the positive relationship between the real wage index, the average monthly wage and government bonds, as well as the results of the assessment between the average monthly wage and the external public debt indicators, allow us to note that in the future, an increase in real wages may contribute to the weakening of the dependence on external public debt in the structure of the state debt of the Republic of Armenia.

Let us also add that during the observed period, the change in state budget revenues, official transfers, and the gross domestic product of the Republic of Armenia had a positive impact on the reduction of external public debt, which are also key factors in the context of debt reduction.[135]

The results of the correlation and Spearman rank correlation coefficient estimates carried out during the study were checked using the Shapiro-Wilk Test, making the realism of the proposed approach to improving the external public debt of the Republic of Armenia more illustrative. According to the results of the Shapiro-Wilk Test, the correlations between the selected variables generally follow a normal distribution, with the exception of the average monthly salary and external public debt indicators, which is a result of the low salary indicators recorded during the observed period (see the test results in Annexes No. 3, 4, 5).

The assumption of normality can be checked using numerous statistical procedures, in particular, parametric tests, since their validity depends on it:[136]

---

[135] Matevosyan A., Grigoryan A. (2023). "APPROACHES TO ASSESSING THE INTERACTION BETWEEN RA FOREIGN STATE DEBT AND MACROECONOMIC INDICATORS", "European University" Collection of Scientific Articles 14 (01), 2023, pp. 11-26

136 Ghasemi, A.; Zahediasl, S. (2012). "Normality Tests for Statistical Analysis: A Guide for Non-Statisticians"; 2012. Int J Endocrinol Metab. 10(2): 486-9. DOI: 10.5812/ijem.3505, available at the following link:https://www.ncbi.nlm.nih.gov/pmc/articles/PMC3693611/

Many statistical procedures[137], including correlation, regression, t-tests, and analysis of variance, especially parametric tests, are based on the assumption that the data follow a normal distribution[138] or Gaussian distribution (named after Johann Carl Gauss 1777–1855), i.e. it is assumed that the populations from which the samples are taken are normally distributed.[139] The assumption of normality is especially important when constructing reference ranges for variables.[140] Normality and other assumptions should be taken seriously,[141] because when these assumptions are not true, it is impossible to draw accurate and reliable conclusions about reality.[142]

Normality tests are additional tools for performing graphical normality assessments. The main tests for normality assessment are the Kolmogorov-Smirnov (K-S) test, the Lillyfors corrected K-S test, the Shapiro-Wilk test, the Anderson-Darling test, the Kramer-von Mises test, etc.[143] Among them K-S[144] and Shapiro-Wilk tests are frequently used tests.[145]

Some researchers recommend the Shapiro-Wilk test as the best choice for testing the normality of data.[146] For this reason, the results of the estimates made during the study were checked using the Shapiro-Wilk test, which is based on the correlation between the data and the corresponding normal scores and provides a

---

[137] Field, A. (2009). *Discovering statistics using SPSS.* 3 ed. London: SAGE publications Ltd. p. 822.

[138] Driscoll, P.; Lecky, F.; Crosby, M. (2000). An introduction to everyday statistics-1. *J Accid Emerg Med.* 17(3):205–11

[139] Pallant, J. *SPSS survival manual, a step by step guide to data analysis using SPSS for windows.* 3 ed. Sydney: McGraw Hill; 2007. pp. 179–200

[140]Royston, P. (1991). Estimating departure from normality. *Stat Med*;10(8):1283–93.

[141]Altman, D.G.; Bland, J.M. (1995). Statistics notes: the normal distribution. *Bmj*;310(6975):298.

[142]Oztuna, D.; Elhan, A.H.; Tuccar, E. (2006). "Investigation of four different normality tests in terms of type 1 error rate and power under different distributions". *Turkish Journal of Medical Sciences*;36(3):171–6

[143]Peat, J.; Barton, B. (2005). *Medical Statistics: A guide to data analysis and critical appraisal.* Blackwell Publishing

[144]Thode, H. J. (2002). *Testing for normality.* New York: Marcel Dekker

[145] Elliott, A.C; Woodward, W. A. (2007). *Statistical analysis quick reference guidebook with SPSS examples.* 1st ed. London: Sage Publications

[146]Thode, H.J. (2002). *Testing for normality.* New York: Marcel Dekker

better, stronger correlation than the K-S test.[147] It is widely believed that investors benefit from global risk sharing and diversification.[148]

Most of the empirical evidence on international investment decisions focuses on stock markets,[149] Relatively less is known about the determinants of bond investment behavior in global markets.[150] With rapid expansion and improved liquidity,[151] as well as ensuring transparency over the past decades [152] Due to their improved risk-return profile, emerging bond markets have become more important in terms of global portfolio allocation.

Fidora[153], Fratscher and Thiemann, Kim et al.[154] have addressed the above questions by presenting evidence on how foreign investors respond to risk-return characteristics in global bond markets. According to Fidora, Fratscher and Thiemann, as well as Kim et al., the available evidence from studies on investment decisions in bond markets shows that risk and return characteristics in the bond market significantly affect households' domestic preferences, and external

---

[147] Steinskog, D. J. (2007). A cautionary note on the use of the Kolmogorov-Smirnov test for normality. *American Meteor Soc.*135:1151–7

[148] Lintner, J. (1965). "Security Prices, Risk, and Maximal Gains from Diversification.". The Journal of Finance 20 (4): 587–615.

[149] See, among others, Dahlquist and Robertsson (2001); Dahlquist et al. (2003); Edison and Warnock (2004); Faruqee, Li, and Yan (2004); Ahearne, Griever, and Warnock (2004); Chan, Covrig, and Ng (2005); Aggarwal, Klapper, and Wysocki (2005); Covrig, Lau, and Ng (2006); Ferreira and Matos (2008); Kho, Stulz, and Warnock (2009).

[150] See, among others, Burger and Warnock (2007); Fidora, Fratzscher, and Thimann (2007); and Horioka, Terada-Hagiwara, and Nomoto (2016)

[151]Bunda, Irina, A. Javier Hamann, and Subir Lall. (2009). "Correlations in Emerging Market Bonds: The Role of Local and Global Factors.", *Emerging Market Review 10 (2): 67–96.*

[152] McGuire, Patrick, and Martijn A. Schrijvers. (2006). "Common Factors in Euro-Denominated Emerging Market Bond Spreads.". *International Finance Review 6: 261–80.*

[153] Fidora, Michael, Marcel Fratzscher, and Christian Thimann. (2007). "Home Bias in Global Bond and Equity Markets: The Role of Real Exchange Rate Volatility. „*Journal of International Money and Finance 26: 631–55.*

[154] Kim, ByoungJoon, Young Sup Yun, BeomCheolCin, and Young Jun Kim. (2014). "Home Bias in Emerging Bond and Stock Markets.". *Emerging Markets Finance and Trade 50 (4): 95–124.*

preferences, according to studies by Horioka[155], Terada-Hagiwara and Nomoto, Burger and Warnock (2007)[156] and (2012)[157].

According to Armenian researcher E. Aghabekyan, the reduction in yields can be considered a positive phenomenon, however, if the latter is not accompanied by changes in relevant economic factors or indicators, it creates certain risks in the future. The risks lie in the overvaluation of bonds by market participants, which can usually be followed by a decline in their prices, which can lead to a certain crisis or instability.[158]

In our opinion, the issue of studying the RA bond market is gaining more importance in the context of the reform of the public debt management concept. For this purpose, it is necessary to take into account the fact that foreign investors are interested in the reliability of the issuer, since the latter pursue a great desire to receive profitability. We consider it necessary to note that the reliability of the issuer is given greater importance among non-resident investors.

Therefore, in order to increase the attractiveness of government bonds, we propose to carry out an active information campaign among potential investors.

Given that foreign participation contributes to liquidity and efficiency in emerging markets, evidence shows that the openness of the capital market will contribute to the development of the bond market, improving the profile of investors and increasing the depth of the market. It should not be forgotten that the basis for providing a promising rating by the largest rating and rating agencies is the precedents of the issues and the stock exchange history of the issuer. At the same time, the return-seeking behavior of foreign investors in emerging bond markets underscores the importance of sound public finances.

---

[155] Horioka, Charles, Akiko Terada–Hagiwara, and TakaakiNomoto (2016). "Explaining Foreign Holdings of Asia's Debt Securities: The Feldstein–Horioka Paradox Revisited."; *Asian Economic Journal 30 (1): 3–24.*

[156] Burger, John D., and Francis E. Warnock. (2007). "Foreign Participation in Local Currency Bond Markets." *Review of Financial Economics 16: 291–304.*

[157] Burger and Warnock's "new angle theory" compares the investment behavior of foreign and domestic investors in global bond markets.

[158] Aghabekyan E., "Are RA Government Bond Yields Overestimated? What to Expect from the Risks Accumulated in the Market?", 2018, available at the following link: https://asue.am/amberd/publications/analytics/profitability-government-bonds-ra-overestimated last accessed on 12.11.2021.

According to Feldstein and Horioka[159], the return-seeking behavior of investors would theoretically lead to a weak correlation between domestic saving and investment rates, but their empirical evidence does not support this argument. This phenomenon is known as the "Feldstein-Horioka puzzle".

Chan, Kovrig, and Ng[160] developed an international asset allocation model that shows that various costs arising from market processes erode the expected returns of foreign investment and lead to a preference for domestic (households) or some foreign investment markets.

Empirical evidence from global stock markets shows that explicit trade barriers, such as capital controls and tax treatment, as well as implicit barriers, such as information asymmetry and investor protection, caused by "bureaucratic" costs, contribute to crowding out investment flows[161].

There are studies in the literature on investment behavior in global bond markets, including those by Fidora, Fratzscher and Thimann, Kim et al. (2014), which focus on risk-return factors.

Fidora, Fratscher, and Thiemann examine the role of real exchange rate volatility in global bond and stock portfolio decisions. They show that real exchange rate volatility significantly explains households' investment preferences in global financial markets, and that real exchange rate volatility reduces households' investment preferences, especially for bond portfolios.

Kim et al. examine foreign investment in global bond and stock markets, finding that market performance has a more pronounced effect than macroeconomic factors on household preferences in both bond and stock markets.

---

[159] Feldstein, M., and Horioka, Ch. (1980). "Domestic Saving and International Capital Flows."; *The Economic Journal 90: 314–29.*

[160] Chan, Kalok, Vicentiu Covrig, and Lilian Ng. (2005). "What Determines the Domestic Bias and Foreign Bias? Evidence from Mutual Fund Equity Allocations Worldwide"; *The Journal of Finance 60 (3): 1495–534.*

[161] See, among others, Faruqee, Li, and Yan (2004); Ahearne et al. (2004); Aggarwal, Klapper, and Wysocki (2005); Chan, Covrig, and Ng (2005); Ferreira and Matos (2008); Kho, Stulz, and Warnock (2009).

Other researchers have examined foreign investor preferences. Burge and Warnock examine 40 global bond markets among U.S. investors and find that they are not well diversified.

Warnock et al.[162] analyzed the factors that attracted U.S. investors to emerging market local currency bonds in 2006 and 2008 and found that U.S. investments were dominated by markets with higher yields, positive skewness, and greater openness.

Horioka, Terada-Hagiawara, and Nomoto studied foreign investment in Asian bond markets and found that foreign investors value higher risk-adjusted returns and lower exchange rate risk when investing in Asian bond markets.

Other studies examine social and political factors, examining how various "bureaucratic" costs associated with social and political factors shape investors' portfolio decisions in bond markets. For example, there are studies that examine investor behavior in relation to factors such as familiarity (Ferreira and Miguel 2011[163]), patriotism, culture, and domestic creditor protection (Pradhan 2016a[164], 2016b[165]), and political constraints and instability (Eichler, Stefan, and Timo Plaga 2017[166]), etc. Foreign and domestic investors may have different preferences in terms of investment horizon, risk appetite, and mandates.

The results of the studied professional literature show that risks arising from economic, political and market factors limit the distribution of global risks and financial integration.[167]

---

162 Warnock, Francis E., and Veronica C. Warnock. (2009). "International Capital Flows and U.S. Interest Rates."; *Journal of International Money and Finance 28 (6): 903–19.*

163 Ferreira, Miguel, and Antonio F. Miguel. (2011). "The Determinants of Domestic and Foreign Bond Bias."; *Journal of Multinational Financial Management 21: 279–300.*

164 Pradkhan, E. (2016a). "Impact of Culture and Patriotism on Home Bias in Bond Portfolios."; *Review of Managerial Science 10 (2): 265–301.*

165 Pradkhan, E. (2016b). "Impact of Domestic Investor Protection on Foreign Investment Decisions: Evidence from Bond Markets."; *International Journal of Finance and Economics 21 (4): 417–46.*

166 Eichler, Stefan, and Timo Plaga. (2017). "The Political Determinants of Government Bond Holdings."; *Journal of International Money and Finance 73 (Part A): 1–21.*

167 Donghyun Park, Kiyoshi Taniguchi, and Shu Tian. (2014). "Foreign and Domestic Investment in Global Bond Markets". *ADB economics working paper series, NO. 535,* available at the following link:https://www.adb.org/sites/default/files/publication/396581/ewp-535-foreign-domestic-investment-bond-markets.pdf

In summary, we note that the trend of increasing integration of bond markets in international capital markets and ensuring an attractive risk-return ratio require additional research, which will be aimed at identifying the factors that have a decisive impact on the preferences, behavior, and investment decisions of resident and non-resident investors.

The results of the above studies will be useful for policymakers and implementers both in improving the positions of profiles in the international capital market and in ensuring the integration participation of private companies.

In recent years, the assessments given to the Republic of Armenia by reputable international organizations are not only encouraging, but also promising. In particular, the rating agency "Fitch Ratings" has reaffirmed the sovereign "B+" rating for the issuance of long-term liabilities in foreign currency of the Republic of Armenia with a stable outlook.[168]

According to Fitch[169], the revision of Armenia's sovereign rating outlook is based on the positive dynamics of the economy and high economic growth, which was positively affected by the significant inflow of people and capital, the overfulfillment of tax revenues and the reduction of the debt burden, and the improvement of the external position of the economy.

In particular, Armenia's high economic growth is noteworthy, which in 2022 was estimated at 11.6%, the highest in the last 15 years. The formation of high growth was influenced by the significant inflow of migrants and capital. The agency expects that a significant part of migrants will remain in Armenia for at least two to three years, which will lead to the maintenance of positive economic developments.

A significant decrease in the budget deficit was also recorded, mainly due to the high growth in tax revenues. As a result, the budget deficit/GDP indicator in 2022 amounted to 2.2% compared to 4.6% in 2021. In addition, the government

---

[168] Fitch ratings (2022). "Fitch Affirms Armenia at 'B+'; Outlook Stable", available at the following link: https://www.fitchratings.com/research/sovereigns/fitch-affirms-armenia-at-b-outlook-stable-18-03-2022

[169] Fitch Ratings (2023). "Fitch Ratings has revised the Outlook on Armenia's Long-Term Foreign-Currency Issuer Default Rating (IDR) to Positive from Stable and affirmed the IDR at 'B+'". available at the following link:https://www.fitchratings.com/research/sovereigns/fitch-revises-armenia-outlook-to-positive-affirms-at-b-10-02-2023

debt in 2022 decreased by almost 13 percentage points, accounting for 47.6% of GDP, and is expected to remain at that level in the medium term.

The improvement in the external position, the current account surplus, amid capital inflows, is also considered positive, which also contributed to an increase in foreign exchange reserves by 880 million USD. In addition, in 2022. net external debt decreased by about 12 percentage points and amounted to 44.5% of GDP.

The agency also noted the factors contributing to the further improvement of the sovereign rating, which are the continuous decrease in the government debt/GDP ratio in the medium term and the maintenance of the external position and financial improvement recorded as a result of significant capital inflows in the medium term.

The analysis shows that the factors influencing investment decisions among foreign investors, such as the stability of the dram, external and internal political stability, the tax field, liberalized economic policy, a free competitive market, etc., are of key importance in the context of increasing investment attractiveness, ensuring economic growth in the Republic of Armenia, as well as reducing the debt burden.

The development of the capital market of the Republic of Armenia, ensuring the progression of participation in the international capital market, and implementing a policy that stimulates exports are of key importance for the structural policy aimed at reducing the burden of public debt. The provision of the aforementioned tools must be combined with the existing fiscal rules, while ensuring fiscal prudence.

In this context, the thesis put forward by us as a result of our previous study that there is a positive relationship between real wages and government bonds[170], therefore, an increase in the volume of government bond purchases in the long term can significantly weaken the RA's dependence on external borrowing in the structure of the public debt, while at the same time reducing the sensitivity to interest rate shocks, which was assessed as high in our previous study

[170] Grigoryan A. (2022). "Manifestations of the Behavior and Exchange Rate Impact of Government Bonds Circulating in the RA Capital Market in the Context of External Public Debt Management", pp. 141-145 ("Region and World" 2022, No. 1) periodical, available at the following link: http://geopolitika.am/dir/wp-content/blogs.dir/1/files/2022_1_141_145.pdf

"Assessment of the RA Public Debt Sustainability Analysis using the International Monetary Fund's MAC DSA Methodology."[171]

Thus, taking into account the fact that the financial and economic situation of the country significantly contributes to the formation of the investment environment, we can state that perceptions of risk towards the country contribute to the crowding out effect of investments. Therefore, in order to increase the economic activity of the Republic of Armenia, ensure real economic growth, and reduce the burden of public debt, it is of key importance for policymakers and implementers to adopt a policy aimed at promoting the investment attractiveness of the Republic of Armenia as a priority in the toolkits for implementing the above-mentioned goals.

3.2 Proposed approach to assessing the optimal level of foreign reserves and the potential for servicing public debt

Quantitative studies of external public debt are not sufficient to assess the efficiency of external debt use. For this reason, one of the research directions we have considered is the assessment of the relationship between debt and economic activity indicators.

We believe that ensuring high-quality economic growth and a high level of employment are necessary prerequisites for reducing dependence on external liabilities, and in this direction, the sectors considered as priorities in the Republic of Armenia are industry, export promotion, tourism development, information technology sector development, and agriculture.

In recent years, due to debt sustainability issues, the Government of the Republic of Armenia has been forced to pursue a restrictive spending policy, as a

---

[171] Matevosyan, A.; Grigoryan, A. (2022). "Assessment of the analysis of the sustainability of the RA public debt according to the MAC DSA methodology of the International Monetary Fund"; *"ADVANCE RESEARCH JOURNAL OF MULTIDISCIPLINARY DISCOVERIES" I Vol.68 I Issue-1 I Chapter-1 E-ISSN : 2456-1045,* available at the following link: http://www.journalresearchijf.com/wp-content/uploads/FM-V68-I1-C1-DEC-2021-PP-01-09.pdf?fbclid=IwAR3RyDu0ls8P9TrJDN4X6-mvWTOd812twXYK_P4uj-RkP9O7zEGI9mjKKYU

[171] Greenidge, K; Craigwell, R; Chrystol, T.; Drakes, L. (2012). "Threshold Effects of Sovereign Debt"

result of which capital investments are being reduced. In this context, we can emphasize that private investments have also been reduced in previous years. Therefore, in the coming years, the Government of the Republic of Armenia will have to allocate more budgetary funds to debt service payments, which may hinder the increase in allocations to other sectors, in particular, capital expenditures.

A number of studies have addressed the issue of the optimal level of external debt-to-GDP ratio. Empirical studies by a number of researchers address the issue, for example, those by Greenidge et al.[172], Menzinger et al.[173], Fay and Thiam[174], Wade[175], Omotosho et al.[176], Adeni et al.[177], Meri et al.[178], Ehikioyan et al.[179], Aziz and N'Zuen[180]. However, there is no consensus on the threshold of external debt to be discussed.

Greenidge et al.[181] studied the marginal effects between public debt and economic growth in the Caribbean. Their study confirmed the existence of a threshold of 55-56% of debt to gross domestic product (GDP). They also found that debt dynamics began to change well before reaching this threshold. In

---

[172] Greenidge, K; Craigwell, R; Chrystol, T.; Drakes, L. (2012). "Threshold Effects of Sovereign Debt: Evidence from the Carribean", *IMF Working Paper. 157, Washington DC.*

[173] Mencinger, J.; Aristovnik, A.; Miroslav, V. (2014). "The Impact of Growing Public Debt on Economic Growth in the European Union". *Amfiteatru Economic Journal* 16(35):403-414.

[174] Faye, I.; Thiam, D. (2015). "Impacts de l'endettement public sur l'économie sénégalaise", *Direction de la Prévision et des Etudes Economiques (DPEE).*

[175] Wade, A. (2015). "Policy-Mix et Croissance Economique dans la Zone UEMOA". *Économies et finances, Université d'Auvergne – Clermont Ferrand I.*

[176] Omotosho, B; Bawa, S.; Doguwa, S. (2016). "Determining the Optimal Public Debt Threshold for Nigeria". *CBN Journal of Applied Statistics* 7(2):1-25

[177] Adeniyi, O.; Adekunle, W.; Orekoya, S. "Non-linear Relation between External Debt and Economic Growth in Nigeria: Does the Investment Channel Matter?" Available at the following link: https://mpra.ub.unimuenchen.de/99975/*MPRA Paper No. 99975*

[178] Mary, F.M.; Sunday, K.E.; Haruna, A.T. (2019). "Optimal Government Debt and Economic Performance in Nigeria". *International Journal of Academic Research in Economics and Management Sciences* 8(3):385-399.

[179] Ehikioya, B.I; Omankhanlen, A.E.; Osuma, G.O.; Inua, O.I. (2020). "Dynamic Relations Between Public External Debt and Economic Growth in African Countries: A Curse or Blessing?". *Journal of Open Innovation: Technology, Market, and Complexity* 6(3):88.

[180] Aziz, D.A; N'Zué, F.F. (2020). "The Ivorian External Debt: Is There a Threshold?". *Journal of Economics and Finance 12(1):01-09.*

[181] Greenidge, K.; Craigwell, R.; Chrystol, T.; Drakes, L. (2012). "Threshold Effects of Sovereign Debt: Evidence from the Carribean". *IMF Working Paper. 157, Washington DC.*

particular, at debt levels below 30% of GDP, an increase in the debt-to-GDP ratio is associated with faster economic growth. However, as debt rises above 30%, the impact on economic growth rapidly declines, and at debt levels that reach 55-56% of GDP, the impact on growth shifts from positive to negative. Thus, beyond this threshold, debt tends to drag on economic growth.

Menzinger et al.[182] studied the direct impact of higher debt on economic growth in the EU-25 countries. They divided the EU countries into subgroups to distinguish between "old" member states, covering the period 1980-2010, and "new" member states, covering the period 1995-2010. Using the panel estimation method, they confirmed the nonlinear relationship between the ratio of public debt per capita and GDP. They also found that the threshold for the debt-to-GDP ratio should be approximately 80 to 90% for "old" member states. However, for "new" member states, the threshold for the debt-to-GDP ratio is lower, at 53 to 54%.

Fey and Thiam use a "nested generation's" model to study the impact of public debt on consumption, GDP, savings, fiscal revenues, investment, and capital dynamics in Senegal. The results show that the A 10% increase in GDP has a positive effect on macroeconomic variables, but worsens the current account deficit. A 10% increase in domestic debt leads to a recession. An increase in government spending financed by debt leads to an increase in government debt bequeathed to future generations by 15% and an increase in future consumption by about 2%.[183]

In this subsection of the book, we have addressed the RA's public debt servicing capacity in collapse situations.

The level of replenishment and adequacy of international reserves of any country allows us to predict the depth of the country's susceptibility to financial and economic collapse situations.

In this context, taking into account the development prospects of the RA, the limited involvement of alternative investment funds, the continuous growth of

---

[182] Mencinger, J.; Aristovnik, A.; Miroslav, V. (2014). "The Impact of Growing Public Debt on Economic Growth in the European Union". *Amfiteatru Economic Journal* 16(35):403-414.
[183] Abdoul Aziz Diallo and Felix Fofana N'Zué. (2021). "An econometric analysis: Is there an optimal external debt threshold for Guinea?". *Journal of Economics and International Finance, Vol. 13(3),* pp. 136-142, July-September 2021 DOI: 10.5897/JEIF2021.1140 Article Number: 540E85567961, pp. 139-140, available at the following link:
https://academicjournals.org/journal/JEIF/article-full-text-pdf/540E85567961

the current level of the RA's external debt due to current geopolitical challenges, in the event of economic shocks, the need for research on the adequacy of the RA's external reserves becomes urgent in order to avoid severe negative consequences and economic shocks.

The research objective of this sub-question of the study was to assess the replenishment and adequacy of the RA's international reserves in conditions of geopolitical uncertainties.

During the study, the task was set to study the level of sufficiency of the RA Central Bank's international reserves as a factor guaranteeing the ability to service external liabilities and mitigating vulnerability.

The methodological basis for assessing the optimal level of Armenia's foreign reserves was the Redi criterion and Guidotti rule, which are widely used in international practice.

During the study, the results of the assessments made according to the Redi criterion and Guidotti rule showed that the current level of Armenia's foreign reserves is assessed as sufficient in the event of unforeseen shocks.

Although many emerging market economies have liberalized some of their foreign financial relations in recent years, most of them maintain a mixed system of restrictions and freedoms related to capital movements.[184]

The term "international liquidity" has been used for several years as a synonym for "international reserves" rather than as a defined functional term as a measure of a country's ability to finance a deficit.[185]

"International reserves" were defined in the Osola report as "assets of a country's monetary authorities" that can be used directly when funds for external payments are in short supply.[186]

---

[184] Kapteyn, A.; de Beaufort W.O., (2001). "Reserve Adequacy in Emerging Market Economies", *IMF Working Paper 01/143, September*, p. 7, available at the following link:https://www.imf.org/external/pubs/ft/wp/2001/wp01143.pdf

[185] Williamson, John. (1973). "International Liquidity: A Survey,"; International Liquidity: Are the Supply and Composition Appropriate? p. 59, available at the following link: https://www.bostonfed.org/-/media/Documents/conference/28/conf28d.pdf

[186] Group of Ten. Report of the Study Group on the Creation of Reserve Assets. 1965, (Ossola Report).

Various approaches are used to assess the adequacy of external reserves, the most common of which are:

1. The ratio of external reserves to import volume, which shows how many months of imports can be covered by reserves in the event of a shock.

2. The ratio of external reserves to short-term external liabilities[187]

3. Foreign reserves must exceed 20 percent of the money supply.

4. The approach used by the International Monetary Fund, according to which export earnings, the monetary base, short-term debt, and other liabilities are used to calculate the minimum level of foreign reserves.[188]

In 2016, the Central Bank of Armenia was classified by the IMF as a floating exchange rate regime central bank[189]. However, before that, in 2014 and 2015[190], the Central Bank of Armenia was classified as a de facto floating fixed exchange rate regime central bank. By the way, the de facto currency regimes adopted by countries often differ from the declared de jure regimes[191]. This discrepancy was called the "fear of floating" by G. Calvo and K. Reinhart. The authors studied and

---

[187] The "Greenspan-Guidotti" rule.

[188] IMF (2016). "Guidance Note on The Assessment of Reserve Adequacy and Related Considerations", *The IMF staff report, June*, p. 25

[189] IMF (2016). "Annual Report on Exchange Arrangements and ExchangeRestrictions 2016", *International Monetary Fund Washington,* p. 7, available at the following link: https://www.imf.org/en/Publications/Annual-Report-on-Exchange-Arrangements-and-Exchange-Restrictions/Issues/2017/01/25/Annual-Report-on-Exchange-Arrangements-and-Exchange-Restrictions-2016-43741

[190] IMF (2015). "Annual Report on Exchange Arrangements and Exchange Restrictions 2015", *International Monetary Fund Washington,* p. 6, available at the following link: https://www.imf.org/en/Publications/Annual-Report-on-Exchange-Arrangements-and-Exchange-Restrictions/Issues/2017/01/25/Annual-Report-on-Exchange-Arrangements-and-Exchange-Restrictions-2015-42751

[191] IMF (2014). "Annual Report on Exchange Arrangements and Exchange Restrictions 2014",*International Monetary Fund Washington,* p. 5, available at the following link: https://www.imf.org/en/Publications/Annual-Report-on-Exchange-Arrangements-and-Exchange-Restrictions/Issues/2016/12/31/Annual-Report-on-Exchange-Arrangements-and-Exchange-Restrictions-2014-41643

presented a number of reasons that explain the phenomenon of "fear of floating[192]".

• in developing countries, the mechanism of transmission from exchange rate to inflation is quite fragmented, therefore, exchange rate stability is considered as the basis for ensuring a low, stable level of inflation,

• distrust in the bodies implementing monetary and currency policy forces them to pay great attention to exchange rate stability,

• exchange rate fluctuations negatively affect foreign trade,

• in developing countries, private and public external liabilities reach large volumes, and sharp fluctuations in foreign exchange rates, especially depreciation, can lead to imbalances in the financial system.

The above reasons raise the question of why countries do not simply declare and implement a fixed exchange rate policy in this case.

Theorists A. Barajas, A. Erikson and R. Steiner presented[193] the following main reasons for the phenomenon of "Fear of Announcement":

• exchange rate flexibility serves as an insurance mechanism for some countries in crisis situations, and by de jure maintaining a floating currency regime, these countries have the opportunity to act more freely in unstable economic situations and have the right not to pay attention to exchange rate fluctuations,

• market participants often do not have the opportunity to identify the differences between the announced and actually implemented policies, therefore, their actions and expectations become more manageable.[194]

---

[192] Hausmann, R.; Panizza, U.; Stein, E., (2000). "Why Do Countries Float the Way theyFloat?", Inter-American Dvelopment bank, *May, Working Paper 418*, pp. 4-5

[193] Barajas, A.; Erickson, A.; Steiner, R., "Fear of Declaring: Do Markets Care What Countries Say About Their Exchange Rate Policies?", *IMF Staff Papers, Vol. 55, No. 3*

[194] Vardanyan, K., J., Avagyan, G., A., Petrosyan, G., A., (2018). "Ensuring a Sufficient Level of International Reserves as a Factor Reducing Economic Vulnerability", Region and World, 2018, No. 4, pp. 85-86, available at the following link:
http://test.journals.sci.am/index.php/region_and_world/article/view/3479/3018

Ensuring the replenishment of foreign reserves of both developed and transition economies is one of the key activities of central banks. In this context, it is important to note that any underperformance by the central banks of the countries in the processes of managing international reserves can lead to serious consequences. However, the primary goal of the Central Bank of the Republic of Armenia is to ensure price stability and financial stability in the country. The main goal of the Central Bank is interconnected with other goals, in particular, from the perspective of the function of managing foreign reserves, a detailed study of the characteristics of exchange rate behavior and external public debt management is important, since the successful management of the Central Bank's international reserves is considered the main indicator of the country's resistance to crisis situations and the weakening of its vulnerability.

According to Armenian researcher K. Atoyan, the Central Bank manages international reserves, guided by the following motives:

- Protection of the national currency. gold standard. International reserves are designed to ensure the protection of the national currency, which mainly refers to official gold reserves.
- Satisfying foreign exchange demand and financing balance of payments deficits: Bretton Woods system. International reserves are sometimes used to satisfy the foreign exchange demand of financial institutions, as well as to finance the current account deficit of the country's balance of payments.
- Intervention: According to the classical definition, intervention is an operation carried out by Central Banks to influence the exchange rate of a currency, which is considered the primary motive for the demand for reserves.
- Wealth accumulation: The Central Bank considers international reserves as the sum of liquid and investment packages. The liquid package should include assets with the highest liquidity, which are mainly designed to insure against the negative gap that arises during interventions, unexpected debt repayments and other unforeseen events. And the goal of managing the investment package is the accumulation of wealth. The Central Bank, using portfolio theory and applied models and having previously determined the permissible level of risk, tries to find the optimal risk/return ratio.
- International reserves are also used to service external liabilities, as well as to combat disasters caused by force majeure. When solving such problems, the availability of reserves is especially important in the case of small

economies, for which force majeure risks can cause a deep crisis: for example, a hurricane in the Caribbean, an earthquake and flood in Japan.[195]

Reserves act as a buffer against economic and financial crises.[196] This is applicable to all countries, particularly emerging and transition economies, whose markets are exposed to shocks from fluctuations in international capital flows.[197]

The Russian-Ukrainian military-political conflict has had negative consequences for the global economic system, international financial and commodity markets, and, naturally, the economy of the Republic of Armenia.

During the conflict, “economic sanctions” were applied to Russia, and restrictions were also imposed on international transfers.

The negative effects of military-political “escalations” on the economy of the Republic of Armenia were perhaps more pronounced, since the predominant part of the Republic of Armenia’s trade turnover is provided by Russian routes. Economic Russian channels were disrupted, international bank transfers became difficult, and “inflation syndromes” were recorded in almost all countries.

Recently, in order to curb inflation in the Republic of Armenia, the country’s main bank has been pursuing a tight money policy. At the meeting of the Board of the Central Bank of the Republic of Armenia held on December 13, 2022, the refinancing rate was increased, setting it at 10.75 percent, and at the first meeting of the Board in 2023 it remained unchanged. The Central Bank of Armenia has been implementing an inflation targeting strategy since 2006.

The Central Bank of Armenia's currency policy is aimed at strengthening the reliability of the Armenian dram and international confidence in it through effective management of foreign exchange reserves, liberalizing currency

---

195 ATOYAN, K., (2015). "INSTITUTIONAL BASIS AND MANAGEMENT FEATURES OF INTERNATIONAL FOREIGN EXCHANGE RESERVES AT THE CURRENT STAGE", BANBER 2015.(3), pp. 10-11, available at the following link: https://hal.science/hal-03284408/document

196 Fisher, S., IMF and World Bank (2001). “International Reserves Management Policies,” conference proceedings, April 28.

197 ATOYAN, K., (2015). "INSTITUTIONAL BASIS AND MANAGEMENT FEATURES OF INTERNATIONAL FOREIGN EXCHANGE RESERVES AT THE CURRENT STAGE", BANBER 2015.(3), p. 12, available at the following link: https://hal.science/hal-03284408/document

operations, and creating a favorable legal and economic framework for foreign investments.

The Central Bank implements a policy of freely floating exchange rates. The Central Bank's intervention in exchange rate formation is limited to instruments of indirect influence.[198]

An important prerequisite for ensuring a stable exchange rate is the necessary saturation with foreign reserves. At the same time, the measurability of foreign reserves is important in the context of assessing the financial stability of the country. According to the World Bank Development Indicators, compiled from officially recognized sources, international reserves (excluding gold) in Armenia amounted to 2940291441 USD in 2022 (see Appendix No. 6).[199]

It is important to emphasize that in 2021, Armenia's international reserves increased by about 23.5 percent compared to the previous year. As a historical overview, we note that the minimum level of replenishment of Armenia's international reserves was recorded in 2014, amounting to 1.489 billion USD.

In 2021, Armenia's international reserves were replenished at the expense of 750 million USD of Eurobonds placed by Armenia in the international capital market on January 26 of the same year. The purpose of the placement was to finance the state budget deficit.

Although the issuance of Eurobonds is considered a successful financial transaction for the Republic of Armenia, since the supply of issues has several times exceeded the demand, which indicates that the foreign world considers the Republic of Armenia to be a reliable partner, nevertheless, one should not give in to the temptation, forgetting that the funds attracted from the international capital market ultimately contribute to both the increase in the burden of the state debt and the allocation of funds for its servicing in the coming years.

Taking into account the huge funds allocated for servicing and repaying the external state debt of the Republic of Armenia in the coming years, especially in 2025 and 2029 according to the Guidotti rule, in the medium term, based on

---

[198] Central Bank of the Republic of Armenia, (2022). "Announcement on the Monetary Policy of the Central Bank of the Republic of Armenia", p. 1, available at the following link: https://www.cba.am/Storage/AM/downloads/karger/Arjutaynhaitarar.pdf
[199] Source: www.tradingeconomics.com

forecast indicators, we have localized the coefficient to assess the average level of the external state debt of the Republic of Armenia.

Figure 12 shows that the repayments of the government's external debt formed at the end of 2021 are spread out until 2054, and the domestic debt until 2050.

According to the Guidotti rule, the country's international reserves should cover the volume of one year's external debt service. That is, the coefficient is calculated by the ratio of short-term external debt to international reserves.

According to the Guidotti rule, we have estimated the average level of the RA external public debt based on the payments on the RA government's debt according to the set of instruments.

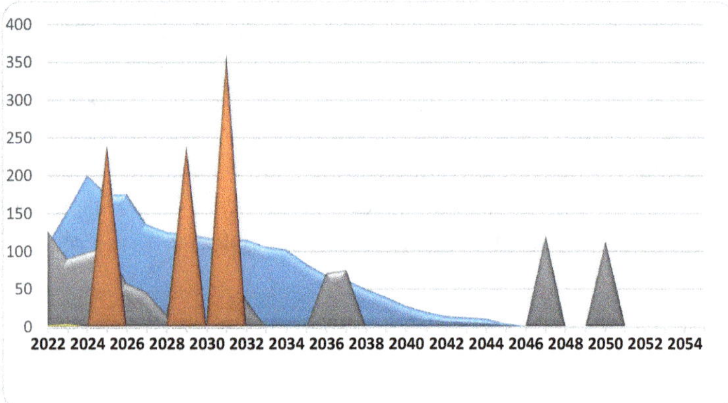

Figure 10. Government debt repayment schedule by instrument as of 31.12.2021 (billion drams)[200]

[200] "RA GOVERNMENT DEBT MANAGEMENT STRATEGIC PLAN FOR 2023-2025", p. 13, available at the following link: https://www.minfin.am/hy/page/partqi_razmavarutyun/

Table 10.

The ratio of the volume of international reserves and external debt service of the Republic of Armenia according to Guidotti's rule [201]

Year	2013	2014	2015	2016	2017	2018	2019	2020	2021	2022
Interest payments (Armenian drams)	98.29	72.66	74.08	98.27	122.1	139.0	157.5	164.7	180.8	198.3
Net international reserves of the Central Bank of Armenia (Armenian drams)[202]	651,793	437,389	568,505	764,309	766,524	765,792	1,071,757	1,058,343	1,186,554	1,287,519
Guidotti coefficient	**15.1**	**16.6**	**13.0**	**12.9**	**15.9**	**18.1**	**14.7**	**15.6**	**15.2**	**15.4**

Calculations by the author.

[201] Data: annual reports on the state debt of the Republic of Armenia.

[202] Summary indicators of the Central Bank of the Republic of Armenia https://www.cba.am/am/sitepages/statsdds.aspx

Guidotti's rule was later revised by the Indian economist Reddy, becoming known as the "Reddy criterion", according to which foreign reserves should meet the amount of three months of imports and the principal and service amounts of the external state debt for a period of one year.

Localizing the "Reddy criterion" for assessing the optimal level of foreign reserves of the Republic of Armenia, we have estimated the ratio of the volume of gross international reserves of the Republic of Armenia to the sum of the volume of foreign debt service of the Republic of Armenia and the volume of imports for 3 months.

$$\frac{\textit{Armenia's external debt service amount} + \textit{3 months of import volume}}{\textit{Armenia's gross international reserves}}$$

The results of the analyses conducted to assess the optimal level of the Republic of Armenia's foreign reserves using the Redi criterion and the Guidotti coefficient indicate that it is more appropriate for the Republic of Armenia to assess the level based on the ratios of imports, foreign debt principal and their servicing costs.

Table 11.

Assessment of the replenishment of the Republic of Armenia's international reserves according to the Reddy criterion[203]

Import volume for 3 months of 2021: January, February, March	**936.4[204]**
Import volume for 3 months of 2021: January, February, March	**180.8[205]**
International reserves	**1,186,554**
Import volume for 3 months of 2022: January, February, March	**1366.2**
Foreign debt service amount	**198.3**
International reserves	**1,287,519**

Calculations by the author.

[203] Data: annual reports on the state debt of the Republic of Armenia.

[204] "MACROECONOMIC AND FISCAL DEVELOPMENTS OF THE REPUBLIC OF ARMENIA IN THE FIRST QUARTER OF 2021", p. 9, available at the following link: https://www.minfin.am/website/images/files/_2021_I%20%203.docx

[205] "State Debt Report" (2021 annual), p. 17, available at the following link: https://minfin.am/hy/page/tarekan_hashvetvutyunner/

Our assessments based on the above indicators are justified, since the Republic of Armenia is primarily an importing country, and the share of external debt in the structure of the state debt is large.

Thus, the results of the assessment of the optimal level of the Republic of Armenia's external reserves using the "Redi criterion" and the Guidotti coefficient substantiate that the current level of the Republic of Armenia's external reserves is assessed as sufficient in the event of unforeseen shocks.[206]

The management of the Republic of Armenia's international reserves is under the control of the Central Bank of the Republic of Armenia. International reserves are aimed at timely and full servicing and repayment of the Republic of Armenia's external debt. For this reason, the accepted rule in international practice is the balancing of the level of the country's international reserves and the amount of borrowed external funds. There are countries that ensure the level of their international reserves several times higher than the volume of external debt, implementing a more reliable currency policy. International reserves can also act as a factor in satisfying demand, contributing to the smooth implementation of imports.

3.3 Approaches to improving the effective management of external public debt

The financial condition of any country becomes evident by the level of its deficit. There are various sources of financing the state budget deficit, but the most applicable is the attraction of external borrowed funds, which ultimately increases the burden of public debt.

Effective management of external public debt is of key importance in the context of financial management.

When making assessments of the external public debt of the Republic of Armenia during the study, we will use the external debt-export ratio toolkit from

[206] MATEVOSYAN, A., & GRIGORYAN, A. (2023). "RA STATE DEBT SERVICING CAPACITY IN COLLAPSE SITUATIONS", Scientific-Educational Center of NAS RA "KATCHAR" SCIENTIFIC PERIODICAL, 2023 (1), Yerevan 2023, pp. 50-62 http://katchar.isec.am/myfiles/files/katchar2023.pdf

the debt assessment coefficients used by the World Bank to classify borrowing countries.

The results of the analysis carried out using the mentioned methodology allow us to state that, in general, the debt ratio of the Republic of Armenia during the observed periods was within the "acceptable" range set by the World Bank, with the exception of the "critical" range recorded in 2009, 2016 and 2021, the causal interpretation of which was presented in the provisions of the dissertation.

Debt issues have always been at the core of the interests and analyses of representatives of the academic world of different periods.

There is no economy that is not involved in the risks of servicing debt obligations. Initially, the concept of debt itself has caused negative perceptions, but the existence of debt has not always manifested itself as a negative phenomenon.

The global recession and the European sovereign debt crisis have sparked heated debates about the effectiveness of fiscal policy and the consequences of rising public debt. Some economists and commentators suggest that the time is right to apply the lessons learned during the Great Depression and that countries should not shy away from expansionary fiscal policies (see, among others, Krugman[207], DeLong and Summers).[208]

Other economists argue that high levels of public debt negatively affect economic growth[209] and that fiscal consolidation is necessary to anchor expectations and restore confidence.[210]

Effective debt management should include a country's borrowing strategy, assessment and determination of official borrowing levels, the formation of an

---

[207] KRUGMAN, P. (2011). "Financing vs. forgiving a debt overhang," *Journal of Development Economics*, 29(3), 253–268: "Self-defeating Austerity," New York Times, July 7

[208] DELONG, B. J. AND SUMMERS, L. H. (2012). "Fiscal Policy in a Depressed Economy" . *Brookings Papers on Economic Activity, Spring*

[209] COCHRANE, J. H. (2011 a, b). "Inflation and Debt," 2011a, *National Affairs, (9), 56–78. (2011b): "Understanding policy in the great recession: Some unpleasant fiscal arithmetic," European Economic Review*, 55(1), 2–30.

[210] Panizza, U., Presbitero A. F. (2013). "Public debt and economic growth in advanced economies: A survey". *Working paper 78, Money and Finance Research group (Mo.Fi.R.) - Univ. Politecnica Marche - Dept. Economic and Social Sciences,* p. 17, available at the following link:https://econpapers.repec.org/paper/ancwmofir/78.htm

appropriate structure and targeted use of borrowed funds and monitoring the effectiveness of their use.[211]

While, earlier literature had a favorable view of debt as a positive contributor to growth (Modigliani,[212] Solberg[213]), Later studies raised concerns about debt dominance. These were reinforced by the debt crises in developing countries in the 1980s and 1990s.[214]

Kumar and Wu[215] find an inverse relationship between initial debt and subsequent growth. At the same time, although the evidence for a negative relationship between public debt and economic growth is strong, the literature still debates whether high debt causes low economic growth, as well as the pathways through which it occurs.[216]

The literature on debt overhang has received a new impetus since the global financial crisis. For example, Reinhart and Rogoff [217] and Baum,[218] Checherita-Westphal and Rother[219] have provided evidence that above certain levels, debt is associated with lower economic growth.

---

[211] Slav'yuk, R. & Slaviuk, N. (2018). "Government debt management: challenges and perspectives.". *Investment Management and Financial Innovations,* 15(3), 143-156. doi:10.21511/imfi.15 (3).2018.12

[212] Modigliani, F. (1961). "Long-Run Implications of Alternative Fiscal Policies and the Burden of the National Debt". *The Economic Journal*, 71, 730-755. https://doi.org/10.2307/2228247

[213]Solberg, R.L. (1988). *"Sovereign Rescheduling: Risk and Portfolio Management". Routledge.*

[214] Moreno-Badia; Marialuz; Paulo Medas; Pranav Gupta and Yuan Xiang. (2020). "Debt is Not Free," *IMF Working Paper 20/1 (Washington: International Monetary Fund).*

[215] Kumar, M., & Woo, J. (2010). "Public Debt and Growth". *Washington DC: International Monetary Fund, Working Paper, WP/10/174,* available at the following link:https://doi.org/10.5089/9781455201853.001

[216] João Tovar Jalles and Paulo Medas. (2022). "Economic Growth After Debt Surges".*International Monetary Fund WP/22/159*p. 4, available at the following link:https://www.imf.org/en/Publications/WP/Issues/2022/07/29/Economic-Growth-After-Debt-Surges-521357

[217] Reinhart, C.M.; Rogoff, K.S. (2010). "Growth in a time of debt. 100(2):573–578, available at the following link:https://www.aeaweb.org/articles?id=10.1257/aer.100.2.573

[218] Baum, A.; Checherita-Westphal, C.; and Rother P. (2013). "Debt and Growth: New Evidence for the Euro Area.". *Journal of International Money and Finance* 32: 809–21

[219] CHECHERITA-WESTPHAL, C. ROTHER, P. (2012). "The Impact of High Government Debt on Economic Growth and Its Channels: An Empirical Investigation for the Euro Area". *European Economic Review, 56, No. 7*, pp. 1392 – 1405.

External debt is an important driver of economic growth and a means of balancing budgets.[220]

The negative impact of external debt on economic growth is stronger than that of domestic debt.[221] Currently, questions about approaches to assessing external public debt have become more relevant in the research and discussions of both foreign authors and reputable international organizations, which determines the relevance of the research.

The research dedicated to assessing the external public debt burden was conducted at the Department of Finance of the Armenian State University of Economics. During the research, the public debt burden assessment indicators used by the World Bank were considered, of which the most appropriate one was identified for the Republic of Armenia.

Debt sustainability is assessed based on debt stock or debt service indicators related to various measures of repayment capacity (usually GDP, exports or state revenues).[222]

To assess the public debt burden, we can use different data sets, each of which reflects different perspectives on the debt burden and public debt sustainability.

The methodological basis for the study was the ratio of external debt to annual export growth rates, used by the World Bank to classify debtor countries. The specified ratio provides an idea of the debtor country's ability to fulfill its obligations on time and in full. Naturally, the more developed the debtor country is, the smaller the ratio calculated for the specified indicators will be, and vice versa.

---

[220] Hadhek Zouhaier, Mrad Fatma. (2014). "Debt and Economic Growth". *International Journal of Economics and Financial Issues Vol. 4, No. 2, pp.440-448 ISSN: 2146-4138p.9,* available at the following link:https://dergipark.org.tr/en/download/article-file/362874

[221] Wani, Nassir Ul Haq and Kabir, Habib. (2016). "An evaluation of relationship between public debt and economic growth: A study of Afghanistan" MPRA Munich Personal RePEc Archive. 19 October, available at the following link:
https://mpra.ub.uni-muenchen.de/75538/1/MPRA_paper_75538.pdf

[222] IMF (2008). "External Debt Statistics: Guide for Compilers and Users: External Debt Sustainability Analysis", p. 2, available at the following link:
http://tffs.org/pdf/edsg/edsgcha14.pdf

$$\textbf{Debt ratio} = \frac{\text{Foreign public debt}}{\text{Annual export volume}} X100\%$$

The following criteria are applicable to the indicator by the World Bank:

≥ 220 – critical

-132-220 – acceptable

≤ 132 – low

The research was based on the works of various foreign authors dedicated to the thresholds for assessing public debt and external public debt, online data collections of the Ministry of Finance of the Republic of Armenia and the Statistical Committee of the Republic of Armenia on export indicators of goods for the observed periods.

At the macro level, the disorder of debt policy leads to a low credit rating of the country, against which the ratings of individual economic entities do not differ, which hinders their advancement in international markets.[223]

While fiscal policy directly affects public debt management, monetary policy can play an important supporting role.[224] However, public debt management is important because the size and maturity of public debt affect future fiscal and monetary policy decisions, therefore, coordination of fiscal and monetary policies becomes inevitable.[225]

Different developing countries have had different GDP growth outcomes during the implementation of export-oriented policies.[226] Each country has its own current economic growth, although its growth rate has shifted from slow and

[223] Silaeva, A., Doronkina, I., Boboshko. (2020). "Macroeconomic Policy as A Condition for The Formation of Corporate Financial Policy". *N. / Vol. 9 Núm.* 25: 182 -189, available at the following link:https://amazoniainvestiga.info/index.php/amazonia/article/view/1119/1019

[224] Moore, W., & Skeete, K. (2010). "The implications of monetary policy shocks for government debt management in Barbados", *CBB Working Paper*

[225] Alzyadat, J. (2021). "Public Debt Management and Macroeconomics Policies Coordination". *Evidence from Jordan. Amazonia Investiga, 9(36)*, 59-7, pp. 2-3, available at the following link:https://doi.org/10.34069/AI/2020.36.12.5

[226] Rodrik, D., &Rodriguez, F. (2010). "Trade Policy and Economic Growth: A Skeptic's Guide to the Cross-National Evidence".

erratic to more dynamic, rapid and continuous rates, especially after the "Industrial Revolution".[227]

In general, the ratio of public debt to export volumes reflects the ratio of outstanding debt at the end of the year to the export indicators of goods and services. The resulting coefficient can be one of the criteria characterizing debt sustainability, allowing policymakers to initiate the necessary interventions aimed at solving problems related to the fulfillment of debt obligations.

The external borrowed funds involved, which form debt stocks, will not constitute an additional burden for the state if they are generated in effective investment directions, since real investments in the economy contribute to an increase in the volume of goods and services.

In general, this also emphasizes the need to monitor debt indicators in medium-term scenarios in order to overcome the limitations of the "picture".[228]

Online data from the RA Statistical Committee on the volume of exports of goods and services and the size of the external debt of the Republic of Armenia during the period under study were used to make assessments of the sustainability of the Republic of Armenia's debt, using the World Bank's debt sustainability coefficient as a research basis.

---

[227] Bashir Al Hemzawi & Natacha Umutoni. (2021). "Impact of exports and imports on the economic growth: A case study of Rwanda from 2006 to 2020", p. 9, available at the following link:http://hj.diva-portal.org/smash/get/diva2:1560984/FULLTEXT01.pdf

[228]IMF (2003). "External Debt Statistics: Guide for Compilers and Users".*Part III: Use of External Debt Statistics - Debt Sustainability: Medium-Term Scenarios and Debt Ratios*, p. 4, available at the following link:https://www.imf.org/external/pubs/ft/eds/eng/guide/file4.pdf

Figure 11. RA External Public Debt / Exports 2009-2022[229]

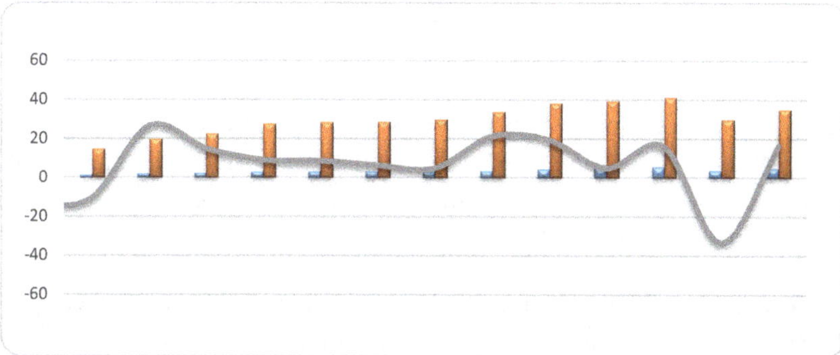

The sharp decline recorded since 2009 was due to the negative consequences of the global financial crisis, which the Armenian economy has not yet overcome, and has faced humanitarian, severe socio-economic problems resulting from the second Artsakh conflict of 2020, as well as the negative challenges of the coronavirus pandemic.

Based on the World Bank criteria (≥ 220 – critical; -132-220 – acceptable; ≤ 132 – low), the results of the analysis provide grounds to conclude that:

- Overall, the debt ratio was within the "acceptable" range during the observed periods.
- In 2010, 2016[230], 2021, the debt ratio was in the "critical" range due to the already mentioned challenges facing Armenia.[231]

The most important factor in ensuring the effectiveness of public debt management is its use in strictly capital-generating directions, which will contribute to ensuring real economic growth, thanks to which the state will be able not only to repay borrowed funds on time, but also to successfully service them.

As a result of the research, it became clear that in 2009 the debt ratio of the Republic of Armenia was within the “critical” range of measurements set by the World Bank, which was a consequence of the negative effects of the global financial and economic crisis, when the Government of the Republic of Armenia was forced to conduct a counter-cyclical fiscal policy, that is, to generate

---

[229] Data are presented in US dollars.

[230] The reduction in Armenia's export volumes as a result of the application of economic sanctions against Russia in 2016 was due to a reduction in export volumes with Russia, its main trading partner.

[231] MATEVOSYAN, A., & GRIGORYAN, A. (2023). “PROPOSED BOARD OF PUBLIC DEBT BURDEN ASSESSMENT”, Alternative scientific journal, ISSN 1829-2828,

additional funds for the real sector at the expense of increasing the deficit in order to counteract the negative macroeconomic effects.

In 2021, the state debt of the Republic of Armenia amounted to 9 billion 226 million USD, increasing by 15.8% compared to the previous year, the bulk of which, 6 billion 643 million USD, was external public debt. The main emphasis of the RA Government's policy aimed at reducing public debt is on ensuring double-digit economic growth and a policy aimed at exports.

The results of the applied research methodology during the observed periods allow us to record that, in general, the RA debt ratio was within the "acceptable" range, which can be considered a positive trend, taking into account the economic uncertainties caused by new geopolitical realities.[232]

In this context, we emphasize the implementation of large state investments by the Government of the Republic of Armenia in capital-generating infrastructure aimed at ensuring economic growth, in combination with large investments in the real sector and stimulating measures aimed at increasing export volumes.

In this part of the dissertation, we have conducted a correlation assessment of the indicators of economic activity and external public debt of the Republic of Armenia, taking into account the fact that the main emphasis in the strategy for reducing the public debt of the Republic of Armenia is on ensuring high economic growth as a vital source of funds for servicing the debt burden.

Since the correlation coefficient obtained as a result of the assessment is -0.37, we can state that the relationship between the economic activity indicator of the Republic of Armenia and external debt indicators during the observed period was assessed as weak, taking into account the low rates of economic activity recorded during the study years.

$$\sigma_x = \sqrt{10946,2 - 10920,3} = 5,1$$

$$\sigma_y = \sqrt{11227,3 - 11193,6} = 5,8$$

$$r_{xy} = \frac{11045,3 - 11056,1}{5,1 \times 5,8} = -\ 0,37$$

---

232 MATEVOSYAN, A., & GRIGORYAN, A. (2023). "PROPOSED BOARD OF PUBLIC DEBT BURDEN ASSESSMENT", Alternative scientific journal, ISSN 1829-2828, 2023 (1), pp. 95-100

Table 12.

Calculation of the correlation coefficient between the RA economic activity index and the RA external debt in percentage terms compared to previous years, 2013-2022.

Year	Economic activity index, compared to the corresponding period of the previous year (%), x	RA external public debt, million USD compared to the corresponding period of the previous year (%), y	X_i^2	X_iY_i	Y_i^2
2013	103,5	104,3	10712,3	10795,1	10878,5
2014	104,1	97,2	10836,8	10118,5	9447,8
2015	103,0	114,1	10609,0	11752,3	13018,8
2016	100,7	111,1	10140,5	11187,8	12343,2
2017	107,7	114,8	11599,3	12364,0	13179,0
2018	105,6	100,4	11151,4	10602,2	10080,2
2019	107,8	104,5	11620,8	11265,1	10920,3
2020	92,5	104,7	8556,3	9684,8	10962,1
2021	105,8	109,7	11193,6	11606,3	12034,1
2022	114,2	97,0	13041,6	11077,4	9409,0
Total	**1044,9**	**1057,8**	**109461,6**	**110453,4**	**112273,0**
Average score	**104,5**	**105,8**	**10946,2**	**11045,3**	**11227,3**

Calculations by the cuthor.

Taking into account the results of the assessment of the above-mentioned variables, we considered it appropriate to also conduct a regression assessment of the RA economic activity index and RA external debt indicators (see the assessment results in Table 13).

$$\begin{cases} 10a_0 + 1044,9a_1 = 1057,8 \\ 1044,9a_0 + 109461,6a_1 = 110453,4 \end{cases}$$

$$\begin{cases} 1048a_0 + 109461,6a_1 = 110857,4 \\ 1044,9a_0 + 109461,6a_1 = 110453,4 \end{cases}$$

$$3,1a_0 = 404$$

$$a_0 = 130,2$$

$$1302 + 1044,9a_1 = 1057,8$$

$$a_1 = -0.24$$

Therefore, the univariate regression model will be:

$$\hat{Y}_x = 130,2 - 0,24x$$

Table 13.

Calculation of regression of the indicators of the RA economic activity index and the RA external debt in percentage terms compared to previous years (2013-2022)

Year	Economic activity index, compared to the corresponding period of the previous year (%), x	RA external public debt, million USD compared to the corresponding period of the previous year (%), y	X_i^2	X_iY_i	$\hat{Y}_x = a_0 + a_1x$
2013	103,5	104,3	10712,3	10795,1	105,4
2014	104,1	97,2	10836,8	10118,5	105,2
2015	103,0	114,1	10609,0	11752,3	105,5
2016	100,7	111,1	10140,5	11187,8	106,0
2017	107,7	114,8	11599,3	12364,0	104,4
2018	105,6	100,4	11151,4	10602,2	104,9
2019	107,8	104,5	11620,8	11265,1	104,3
2020	92,5	104,7	8556,3	9684,8	108,0
2021	105,8	109,7	11193,6	11606,3	104,8
2022	114,2	97,0	13041,6	11077,4	102,8
Total	**1044,9**	**1057,8**	**109461,6**	**110453,4**	**1051,2**

Calculations by the author.

Thus, the change in the RA economic activity index will lead to a change in the RA public debt of -0.24%. Taking into account the fact that the appreciation of the dram during 2022 significantly contributed to the successful servicing of the RA debt, which has become more expensive in recent years due to the increase in funds allocated to servicing the domestic debt, in this sub-question of the dissertation work, we have carried out an assessment between the foreign exchange rate (US dollar) and the RA external public debt indicators. The results of the assessment are presented below:

$$\sigma_x = \sqrt{10207,3 - 10160,6} = 6,8$$

$$\sigma_y = \sqrt{11227,3 - 11193,6} = 5,8$$

$$r_{xy} = \frac{10690,1 - 10664,6}{6,8 \; x \; 5,8} = 0,65$$

As a result of the assessment, we obtained a correlation coefficient of 0.65, we can state that the relationship between the dollar exchange rate and the RA external public debt indicators is noticeable.

Table 14.

Calculation of the correlation coefficient of the dollar exchange rate in the RA and the RA external debt indicators in percentage terms compared to previous years for 2013-2022

Year	Foreign exchange rates, AMD / 1 USD average exchange rate compared to the corresponding period of the previous year (%), x	RA external public debt, million USD compared to the corresponding period of the previous year (%), y	X_i^2	X_iY_i	Y_i^2
2013	100,00	104,3	10000,0	10430,0	10878,5
2014	101,54	97,2	10310,4	9869,7	9447,8
2015	114,91	114,1	13204,3	13111,2	13018,8
2016	100,54	111,1	10108,3	11170,0	12343,2
2017	100,46	114,8	10092,2	11532,8	13179,0
2018	100,06	100,4	10012,0	10046,0	10080,2
2019	99,47	104,5	9894,3	10394,6	10920,3
2020	101,78	104,7	10359,2	10656,4	10962,1
2021	103,02	109,7	10613,1	11301,3	12034,1
2022	86,48	97,0	7478,8	8388,6	9409,0
Total	1008,3	1057,8	102072,5	106900,6	112273,0
Average score	100,8	105,8	10207,3	10690,1	11227,3

Calculations by the author.

Taking into account the results of the correlation assessment between the selected variables, we considered it appropriate to also conduct a regression assessment on the dollar exchange rate in the Republic of Armenia and the indicators of the Republic of Armenia's external debt.

$$\begin{cases} 10a_0 + 1008,3a_1 = 1057,8 \\ 1008,3a_0 + 102072,5a_1 = 106900,6 \end{cases}$$

$$\begin{cases} 1012a_0 + 102072,5a_1 = 107049,4 \\ 1008,3a_0 + 102072,5a_1 = 106900,6 \end{cases}$$

$$3,7a_0 = 148,8$$

$$a_0 = 40,2$$

$$402 + 1008,3a_1 = 1057,8$$

$$a_1 = 0,65$$

Therefore, the univariate regression model will be:

$$\hat{Y}_x = 40,2 + 0,65x$$

Thus, a change in the dollar exchange rate in the Republic of Armenia will lead to a 0.65% change in the Republic of Armenia's public debt.

Summarizing the results of the correlation and univariate regression methods between the selected variables, we have performed multiple correlation and regression estimates between economic activity, foreign exchange rate (USD) and external public debt indicators in the Republic of Armenia. The estimation results are presented in Table 15 and Table 16.

Table 15.

Calculation of regression of the indicators of the exchange rate of the Armenian dollar and the Armenian external debt in percentage terms compared to previous years, 2013-2022

Year	Foreign exchange rates, AMD / 1 USD average exchange rate compared to the corresponding period of the previous year (%), x	RA external public debt, million USD compared to the corresponding period of the previous year (%), y	X_i^2	X_iY_i	$\hat{Y}_x = a_0 + a_1x$
2013	100,00	104,3	10000,0	10430,0	105,2
2014	101,54	97,2	10310,4	9869,7	106,2
2015	114,91	114,1	13204,3	13111,2	114,9
2016	100,54	111,1	10108,3	11170,0	105,6
2017	100,46	114,8	10092,2	11532,8	105,5
2018	100,06	100,4	10012,0	10046,0	105,2
2019	99,47	104,5	9894,3	10394,6	104,9
2020	101,78	104,7	10359,2	10656,4	106,4
2021	103,02	109,7	10613,1	11301,3	107,2
2022	86,48	97,0	7478,8	8388,6	96,4
Total	1008,3	1057,8	102072,5	106900,6	1057,4

Calculations by the author.

Table 16.

Calculation of the multiple correlation between Armenia's economic activity, the dollar exchange rate, and Armenia's external public debt, 2013 - 2022

Year	Economic activity index, compared to the corresponding period of the previous year (%), X_1	Foreign exchange rates, AMD / 1 USD average exchange rate compared to the corresponding period of the previous year (%), X_2	RA external public debt, million USD compared to the corresponding period of the previous year (%), Y	X_1^2	X_1X_2	X_1Y	X_2^2	X_2Y
2013	103,5	100,00	104,3	10712,3	10350,0	0795,1	10000,0	10430,0
2014	104,1	101,54	97,2	10836,8	10570,3	10118,5	10310,4	9869,7
2015	103,0	114,91	114,1	10609,0	11835,7	11752,3	13204,3	13111,2
2016	100,7	100,54	111,1	10140,5	10124,4	11187,8	10108,3	11170,0
2017	107,7	100,46	114,8	11599,3	10819,5	12364,0	10092,2	11532,8
2018	105,6	100,06	100,4	11151,4	10566,3	10602,2	10012,0	10046,0
2019	107,8	99,47	104,5	11620,8	10722,9	11265,1	9894,3	10394,6
2020	92,5	101,78	104,7	8556,3	9414,7	9684,8	10359,2	10656,4
2021	105,8	103,02	109,7	11193,6	10899,5	11606,3	10613,1	11301,3
2022	114,2	86,48	97,0	13041,6	9876,0	11077,4	7478,8	8388,6
Total	1044,9	1008,26	1057,8	109461,6	105179,3	110453,4	102072,5	106900,6
Average score	104,5	100,8	105,8	10946,2	10517,9	11045,3	10207,3	10690,1

Calculations by the author.

$$\sigma_{X_1} = \sqrt{\overline{X_1^2} - \overline{(X_1)}^2}$$

$$\sigma_{X_2} = \sqrt{\overline{X_2^2} - \overline{(X_2)}^2}$$

$$\sigma_y = \sqrt{\overline{Y^2} - \overline{(Y)}^2}$$

$$r_{xy} = \frac{\overline{XY} - \overline{X}\overline{Y}}{\sigma_x \sigma_y}$$

$$r_{y(X_1X_2)} = \sqrt{\frac{r_{X_1Y}^2 + r_{X_2Y}^2 - 2r_{X_1Y}r_{X_2Y}r_{X_1X_2}}{1 - r_{X_1X_2}^2}}$$

Let's do all the necessary calculations.

$$\sigma_{X_1} = \sqrt{10946,2 - 10920,3} = 5,1$$

$$\sigma_{X_2} = \sqrt{10207,3 - 10160,6} = 6,8$$

$$\sigma_y = \sqrt{11227,3 - 11193,6} = 5,8$$

$$r_{X_1y} = \frac{11045,3 - 11056,1}{5,1 \times 5,8} = -0,37$$

$$r_{X_2y} = \frac{10690,1 - 10664,6}{6,8 \times 5,8} = 0,65$$

$$r_{X_1X_2} = \frac{10517,9 - 10533,5}{5,1 \times 6,8} = -0,45$$

$$r_{y(X_1X_2)} = \sqrt{\frac{0,14 + 0,42 - 0,22}{1 - 0,2}} = 0,65$$

Thus, we obtained a multiple correlation coefficient of 0.65, which means that the relationship between the RA economic activity index, the dollar exchange rate, and the RA state external debt is noticeable.

Table 17.

Multiple regression calculation of Armenia's economic activity, dollar exchange rate, and Armenia's external public debt, 2013 - 2022.

Year	Economic activity index, compared to the corresponding period of the previous year (%), X_1	Foreign exchange rates, AMD / 1 USD average exchange rate compared to the corresponding period of the previous year (%), X_2	RA external public debt, million USD compared to the corresponding period of the previous year (%), Y	X_1^2	X_1X_2	X_1Y	X_2^2	X_2Y	$\hat{Y}_x$
2013	103,5	100,00	104,3	0712,3	10350,0	10795,1	10000,0	10430,0	06,5
2014	104,1	101,54	97,2	0836,8	10570,3	10118,5	10310,4	9869,7	07,6
2015	103,0	114,91	114,1	0609,0	11835,7	11752,3	13204,3	13111,2	16,8
2016	100,7	100,54	111,1	140,5	10124,4	11187,8	10108,3	11170,0	06,5
2017	107,7	100,46	114,8	1599,3	10819,5	12364,0	10092,2	11532,8	07,2
2018	105,6	100,06	100,4	1151,4	10566,3	10602,2	10012,0	10046,0	06,7
2019	107,8	99,47	104,5	1620,8	10722,9	11265,1	9894,3	10394,6	06,5
2020	92,5	101,78	104,7	556,3	9414,7	9684,8	10359,2	10656,4	06,6
2021	105,8	103,02	109,7	1193,6	10899,5	11606,3	10613,1	11301,3	08,8
2022	114,2	86,48	97,0	3041,6	9876,0	11077,4	7478,8	8388,6	8,1
Total	**1044,9**	**1008,26**	**1057,8**	**09461,6**	**105179,3**	**110453,4**	**102072,5**	**106900,6**	**071,3**

Calculations by the author.

$$\begin{cases} na_0 + a_1 \sum X_1 + a_2 \sum X_2 = \sum Y \\ a_0 \sum X_1 + a_1 \sum X_1^2 + a_2 \sum X_1 X_2 = \sum X_1 Y \\ a_0 \sum X_2 + a_1 \sum X_1 X_2 + a_2 \sum X_2^2 = \sum X_2 Y \end{cases}$$

$$\begin{cases} \mathbf{10a_0 + 1044,9a_1 + 1008,26a_2 = 1057,8} \\ \mathbf{1044,9a_0 + 109461,6a_1 + 105179,3a_2 = 110453,4} \\ \mathbf{1008,26}a_0 + 105179{,}3a_1 + 102072{,}5a_2 = 106900{,}6 \end{cases}$$

$$a_0 = 26{,}1$$

$$a_1 = 0{,}1$$

$$a_2 = 0{,}7$$

Therefore, the multivariate regression model will be:

$$\hat{Y}_x = 26{,}1 + 0{,}1X_1 + 0{,}7X_2$$

- Multiple regression calculations show that fluctuations in the RA economic activity index and the dollar exchange rate lead to a change in the RA external public debt of 0.1 and 0.7 percent, respectively.
- The results of the assessments made in this sub-question of the dissertation are summarized in the following main approaches:
- The relationship between the RA economic activity index and external public debt indicators in the observed period is weak in the results of the assessment using correlation and regression coefficients.
- The relationship between the foreign exchange rate (US dollar) and the RA external public debt indicators is noticeable in the results of the assessment using correlation and regression coefficients.
- The relationship between the RA economic activity index, the dollar exchange rate and the RA external public debt is noticeable in the results of the assessment using multiple correlation and multiple regression

CONCLUSIONS

- Summarizing the conclusions arising from the scientific and methodological studies conducted during the dissertation, the following main emphases were made.
- Studying the global experience of debt management, we believe that legislative provisions on other indicators can contribute to the improvement of external debt management, in particular, the need to legislatively establish a safety margin for expenditures directed at debt service and repayment.
- In the structure of the RA state debt, external public debt constitutes the overwhelming majority, therefore, in order to weaken the specific weight of external debt in the debt structure, it is necessary to implement an effective information-marketing policy promoting the acquisition of state treasury bonds, taking into account the fact that the history of the RA stock exchange and precedents of issuances indicate that from the perspective of foreign investors, RA state bonds are quite attractive.
- Due to the specific weight of external debt in the structure of the RA state debt, we emphasize the need to conduct additional multifaceted analyses, including from the perspective of ensuring transparency of the decisions of the Government to attract external public debt, directions of use, as well as the policy being implemented.
- Based on the approaches to assessing the sustainability of the RA public debt using the IMF and WB MAC DSA (Debt sustainability analysis for market-access countries) methodology, we can note that although the RA public debt has been assessed as stable, it is nevertheless sensitive to exchange rate and refinancing risks. Therefore, in order to keep risks within manageable limits, we emphasize the development of the domestic borrowing market as a strategic objective.
- We assessed the RA external public debt using the external debt/export ratio toolkit from the debt assessment factors used by the WB to classify borrowing countries, as a result of which the RA debt ratio was in the "acceptable" range, which is a positive trend.
- We effectively implemented the assessment according to Guidotti's rule during the assessment of the optimal level of RA external reserves, the results of which indicate the sufficient replenishment of RA reserve

funds.

- Based on the results of the assessment of the state debt service capacity using the Reddy criterion, we substantiated that the current level of RA foreign reserves is considered sufficient in the event of collapse situations.
- In the results of the Shapiro–Wilk test, the distributions of RA economic activity, foreign exchange rate, and RA external public debt were assessed as normal, since the clusters of RA economic activity and foreign exchange rate changes affect the RA external public debt ratio and the Shapiro–Wilk tests did not show any significant deviation from normality.
- As a result of the multiple linear regression analysis, the growth of the RA economic activity index and the appreciation of the national currency due to foreign exchange fluctuations in the context of the dynamics of the RA external public debt and the decrease in the debt-GDP ratio were assessed as positive during the observed period.
- According to the results of the conducted correlation and regression coefficients, the relationship between the RA economic activity index and external public debt indicators during the observed period was assessed as weak.
- The relationship between the US dollar and the RA external public debt indicators in the RA is noticeable in the results of the correlation and regression coefficients.
- The relationship between the RA economic activity index, the dollar exchange rate and the RA external public debt is noticeable in the results of the multiple regression and correlation evaluation.

REFERENCES

1. Kant, I., (2002) "Groundwork for the Metaphysics of Morals", trans. A. W. Wood, Yale University Press, New Haven, p. 39

2. Stefanutti, S. (2020). of the Philosophy of Debt: In Search of the Relationship Between Debts and Duties, No (2020) https://doi.org/10.7413/24208914074

3. Santner E. & Schuster A. (2016-2017 Autumn) "The debt drive: Philosophy, psychoanalysis, neoliberalism", Retrieved October 3, 2022 available at the following link:
https://english.uchicago.edu/courses/debt-drive-philosophy-psychoanalysis-neoliberalism

4. Douglas, A., X. (2016a.). "The philosophy of debt", *Routledge. Retrieved October 3, 2022, available at the following link:* https://www.thinkingfaith.org/-articles/philosophy-debt

5. Rusyaykina, A. M. (2001) Penza, Public debt management., p.11.

6. Philosophy of Economics (2003/2018) In Stanford Encyclopedia of Philosophy. Retrieved October 3, 2022 available at the following link: https://plato.stanford.edu/entries/economics/

7. Lawson, T. (2016). "The philosophy of debt": The Philosophers Magazine: 10.5840/tpm20167223 available at the following link:
https://www.researchgate.net/publication/296687370_The_philosophy_of_debt p.17

8. Makaryan, A., Hayrapetian A. (2021). "State debt threshold indicators. International research and armenian reality", Proceedings of the Armenian State University of Economics, 4/2021, available at the following link: https://arar.sci.am/dlibra/publication/321590/edition/294748/content

9. Aristotle (1984) Politics J. Barnes. "The Complete Works of Aristotle": Book 1, section1252a: Princeton University Press, available at the following link: http://www.perseus.tufts.edu/hopper/text?doc=urn:cts:greekLit:tlg0086.tlg035.perseus-eng1

10. Shiller, R. J., (2012). "*Finance and the Good Society*", Princeton: Princeton University Press.

11. Philosophy of Money and Finance (2018). In Stanford Encyclopedia of Philosophy. Retrieved October 3, 2022 available at the following link: https://plato.stanford.edu/entries/money-finance/

12. Douglas, A. X. (2020). "What do I owe? The philosophy of debt": Article updated on: 20 January 2020, available at the following link: https://www.iwoca.co.uk/insights/philosophy-of-debt-part-one/
13. Douglas (2015). "The Philosophy of Debt": 23 November, available at the following link:
https://www.taylorfrancis.com/books/mono/10.4324/9781315681009/philosophy-debt-alexander-douglas
14. Heifetz, B. A. (2022). "Gosudarstvennyi dolg" (Public debt in Russian), In Bol'shaya rossiiskaya entsiklopediya (Great Russian Encyclopedia, in Russian) Retrieves October 3, available at the following link:
15. https://bigenc.ru/economics/text/2373368
16. Fedoov, V.M., Buryak L.D., Butakov D.D. (1991) ed. Fedosova V.M. Ogorodnik S.Y a and Sutormina V. N. – K Lybid, Public finance Proc. A manual for students of economic universities and faculty / 1991.–276 p. ISBN 5-11-001607-0. available at the following link:
17. https://kneu.edu.ua/ua/science_kneu/%20scientific_schools/spf/spf_praci/spf_prazi/gosfin/
18. McConnell, K. R. (1992). "Economics: Principles, probl. and Politics": In 2 vols. Vol. 1 / K. R. McConnell, S. L. Brue. M.: Respublika, p. 365
19. Dolan, E. J., (1999). "Money, banking and monetary policy". E. J. Dolan, C. D. Campbell, R. J. Campbell, trans. from English V. V. Lukashevich and others. St. Petersburg: St. Petersburg Orchestra. p. 402
20. Kirakosyan, G. E., Ghushchyan H. B., Tigranyan I. T. (1999) Economic Explanatory Dictionary, Yerevan, Economist, pp. 342-343.
21. Avetisyan, I. A. (2001). "Fundamentals of financial management at the macro level" (questions of theory and methodology). Vologda, p. 194
22. RA Law "On State Debt", 2008 article 5, article 6, available at the following link: https://www.arlis.am/documentview.aspx?docid=119085
23. Vardanyan, K., Avagyan G. & Karapetyan N. (2021). "INTERPRETATION OF THE THEORIES AND THE RESULTS OF EMPIRICAL RESEARCH ON PUBLIC DEBT MANAGEMENT AND THE IMPACT OF DEBT ON ECONOMIC GROWTH. PUBLIC ADMINISTRATION" 1/2021, available at the following link: https://paara.am/wp-content/uploads/2012/06/qnarik-vardanyan-gayane-avagyan.pdf
24. Backhouse, R. & Fontaine P. (Eds., (2010). "The Unsocial Social Science? Economics and Neighboring Disciplines since 1945", Durham, NC: Duke University Press

25. Reinhart, C. M., Rogoff. K. S., Savastano, M. A. (2003). "DEBT INTOLERANCE.NATIONAL BUREAU OF ECONOMIC RESEARCH". Working Paper 9908. http://www.nber.org/papers/w9908
26. Kyurumyan, A. (2014). "Thepolicy decisions and consequenceson public debt management in recent years", p. 53, available at the following link: https://www.osf.am/wp-content/uploads/2014/04/Debt-Managment_Artak-Kyurumyan.pdf
27. Yared, P (2019), "Rising Government Debt: Causes and Solutions for a Decades-Old Trend," *Journal of Economic Perspectives* 33(2): pp. 115-140.
28. Sandleris, G. (2016), "The Costs of Sovereign Defaults: Theory and Empirical Evidence," *Economia* 16(2): 1-27
29. Reinhart, Rogoff, Savastano (2003), Bosher (1970), Vives (1969), Winkler (1933) and Wynne (1951)
30. Eden, Maya, Kraay Aart & Qian Rong. (2012). "Sovereign Defaults and Expropriations Empirical Regularities". The World Bank Policy Research Working Paper 6218.
31. Bi, Huixin, Shen, Wenyi and Yang, Shu-Chun (2014). "Fiscal Limits, External Debt, and Fiscal Policy in Developing Countries". IMF Working Paper #49. March 2014
32. Stiglitz, J. E. (2002). "Globalization and its Discontent". W. W. Norton and company
33. Stiglitz, J. E. (2007). "Making the Globalization Work". W. W. Norton and company.
34. World Bank. (2007). "Managing Public Debt". from Diagnostics to Reform Implementation
35. Zou, F. (2019). "Analysis and Research on Local Government Debt Problems in China". Modern Economy, 10, pp.188-197
https://doi.org/10.4236/me.2019.101013
https://www.scirp.org/pdf/ME_2019011716224598.pdf
36. Kalantari, Sh. & Sholes I. (2019). available at the following link:
37. https://www.philosophytalk.org/shows/ethics-debt
38. Tobin, J. (1963). "An Essay on Principles of Debt Management". N.Y., Cowles Foundation for Research in Economics at Yale University, p. 210
39. Hansen, E. (1997). "Economic cycles and national income. Keynesian Classics" (vol. 2). -M.: p.334
40. Bayadyan, A. & Markosyan H. (2014). "The goals of public debt management and the issues of its regulation". NAS of RA, Current issues of socio-economic

development in the Republic of Armenia #1/2014, pp. 45-49 1829-4324. Available at the following link:
https://arar.sci.am/dlibra/publication/280667/edition/257694/content
41. Chinaryan, V. (2012). "State debt and its management issues". National Academy of Sciences of the Republic of Armenia Current issues of socio-economic development in the Republic of Armenia #2/2012 pp. 106-109. available at the following link:
https://arar.sci.am/dlibra/publication/280508/edition/257543/content
42. Larch, M. (2022). "The (un) sustainability of public debt: the elusive reality of an intuitive concept". Head of Secretariat, European Fiscal Board, 5 April, pp. 25-26, available at the following link:
https://www.coleurope.eu/sites/default/files/research-paper/BEERpaper_41%20Larch%205%20April.pdf
43. RA Ministry of Finance and Statistical Committee
44. RA GOVERNMENT DEBT BURDEN REDUCTION PROGRAM 2022-2026 p. 4
45. MATEVOSYAN, A. & GRIGORYAN, A. (2022). "The Philosophy of External Public Debt Management". *WISDOM*, *24*(4), 91–101 https://doi.org/10.24234/wisdom.v24i4.945 available at the following link: https://wisdomperiodical.com/index.php/wisdom/article/view/945
46. HAKOBYAN E. N., (2016). "THE IMPACT OF STATE DEBT POLICY ON ECONOMIC GROWTH (ISSUES OF THEORY AND PRACTICE)", Phd THESIS for the degree of Candidate of Economics in the specialty "General Economics", pp. 6-7, available at the following link
http://councils.ysu.am/pdf_files/015/2016/015-Eduard_Hakobyan.pdf
47. Melikyan S., (2013). "Features of the Formation and Management of the RA State Debt", p. 7, available at the following link
http://library.asue.am/books/2791.pdf
48. Kyurumyan A., (2014). "Political decisions made in recent years regarding public debt management and their consequences", p. 4, available at the following link: https://www.osf.am/wp-content/uploads/2014/04/Debt-Managment_Artak-Kyurumyan.pdf
49. Carmen M. Reinhardt and Kenneth S. Rogoff. (2009). "This Time is Different: Eight Centuries of Financial Folly", (*Princeton: Princeton, NJ*
50. Austin, A. (2015). "The Debt Limit: History and Recent Increases, Analyst in Economic Policy". p. 27, available at the following link
https://sgp.fas.org/crs/misc/RL31967.pdf

51. Григорян, А. (2022). “ТЕОРЕТИКО-МЕТОДИЧЕСКИЕ ОСНОВЫ УПРАВЛЕНИЯ ВНЕШНИМ ГОСУДАРСТВЕННЫМ ДОЛГОМ РА И ЗАРУБЕЖНЫЙ ОПЫТ”; *(Регион и мир, 2022, № 3), с. 129-132, available at the following link:*
52. http://geopolitika.am/dir/wpcontent/blogs.dir/1/files/2022_3_127_133.pdfSource: www.statista.com
53. HAKOBYAN, E. (2015). "THE BURDENS OF PUBLIC DEBT IN THE WORLD: CHALLENGES OF THE 21ST CENTURY", KNOWLEDGE, INNOVATION AND DEVELOPMENT, Proceedings of the 25th ASUE SCIENTIFIC CONFERENCE, 2015. November 11-13, pp. 169-171, available at the following link:
https://asue.am/upload/files/II_Baj._tarmacvac.pdf
54. IMF (2015). “Lessons from the Crisis in Argentina”. available at the following link:https://bit.ly/3d4EVAP
55. Horvath, J. (2009). “2008 Hungarian Financial Crisis”. CASE Network E-briefs. Najdeno 1. junija 2016 na spletnem naslovu: available at the following link: http://www.case-research.eu/upload/publikacja_pUUUlik/23686666_E-brief_012009%20FINAL.pdf
56. "LUYS Foundation", (2021). "THE POSSIBILITY OF ECONOMIC COLLAPSE IN ARMENIA: MYTH OR REAL THREAT?". pp. 34-47, available at the following link
57. https://www.luys.am/img/artpic/small/5330d854e7677d361266%D5%8F%D5%B6%D5%BF%D5%A5%D5%BD%D5%A1%D5%AF%D5%A1%D5%B6%D5%AF%D5%B8%D5%AC%D5%A1%D5%BA%D5%BD--07-07-2021-edited.pdf
58. Sargsyan K., (2016). "Issues of Increasing the Efficiency of State Anti-Crisis Policy" Yerevan: "Science" Publishing House of the NAS of the Republic of Armenia, 2016, pp. 282-283
59. Wyplosz, Ch. (2007). "Debt Sustainability Assessment: The IMF Approach and Alternatives," *IHEID Working Papers 03-2007, Economics Section, The Graduate Institute of International Studies.,* available at the following link:https://ideas.repec.org/p/gii/giihei/heiwp03-2007.html
60. Foncerrada, L. (2005). “Public debt sustainability. Notes on debt sustainability, development of a domestic governmet securities market and financial risks”, *Análisis Económico, vol. XX, núm. 44, segundo cuatrimestre, p. 11,* available at the following link:
https://www.redalyc.org/pdf/413/41304409.pdf

61. IMF (2021). "Republic of Armenia: 2021 Article IV Consultation, Fourth and Fifth Reviews Under the Stand-By Arrangement, and Request for Waiver of Nonobservance of Performance Criterion and Monetary Policy Consultation Clause-Press Release"; *Staff Report; and Statement by the Executive Director for the Republic of Armenia",* available at the following link:
https://www.imf.org/en/Publications/CR/Issues/2021/12/21/Republic-of-Armenia-2021-Article-IV-Consultation-Fourth-and-Fifth-Revies-Under-the-Stand-511248
62. Bayadyan, A. H., Markosyan H. A. (2015). "The problems of public debt management and ways to solve them in the Republic of Armenia". "Science" Publishing House of the National Academy of Sciences of the Republic of Armenia, pp. 58-59
63. The RA Law "On State Debt", Article 2, is available at the following link: https://www.arlis.am/documentview.aspx?docid=49156
64. IMF and World Bank. (2009). "Managing Public Debt: Formulating Strategies and Strengening Institutional Capacity". p. 8
65. Ministry of Finance of Georgia, (2021). "External Government debt portfolio (31 Dec 2021) represents 80% of the total Government debt", available at the following link: https://www.mof.ge/en/4409
66. Ministry of Finance of Georgia, (2023). "General Government Debt Management Strategy 2023-2026". pp. 2, 9, available at the following link: https://www.mof.ge/images/File/sagvalebi/2023/20-01-2023/1/Government%20Debt%20Management%20Strategy%202023-2026%20-%20Presentation.pdf
67. Central Bank of the Russian Federation, (2023). "Monetary Policy Guidelines for 2020–2022", available at the following link:
68. https://www.cbr.ru/eng/publ/ondkp/on_2020_2022/page/
69. Atanasovska, Yu.V.; Sanginova, L.D.; Balynin, I.V. (2020). "State Debt Management in the Russian Federation in Modern Socio-Economic Conditions" *Advances in Economics, Business and Management Research, volume 138 2nd International Scientific and Practical Conference "Modern Management Trends and the Digital Economy: from Regional Development to Global Economic Growth" (MTDE 2020),*
https://doi.org/10.2991/aebmr.k.200502.212 pp. 1279-1280, available at the following link: https://www.atlantis-press.com/proceedings/mtde-20/125939842
70. Central Bank of the Russian Federation, (2023). "Monetary Policy Guidelines for 2022–2024". pp. 16-17, available at the following link:

71. https://www.cbr.ru/content/document/file/126065/on_project_2022(2023-2024)_eng.pdf
72. Russia External Debt, (2023), available at the following link https://www.ceicdata.com/en/indicator/russia/external-debt
73. Source: WWW.CEICDATA.COM | CEIC Data
74. What was Russia's Government Debt: % of GDP in Mar 2023? available at the following link:
https://www.ceicdata.com/datapage/en/indicator/russia/government-debt--of-nominal-gdp
75. Georgia External Debt, (2023). available at the following link: https://www.ceicdata.com/datapage/en/indicator/georgia/external-debt
76. Georgia Government Debt: % of GDP
https://www.ceicdata.com/datapage/en/indicator/georgia/government-debt--of-nominal-gdp
77. Movsisyan, Sh., (2018). "Problems of Debt Security of the RA Economy", ECONOMY AND SOCIETY DEVELOPMENT. Challenges and Opportunities of the 21st Century. Proceedings of the 27th ASUE Conference / ASUE. - Yerevan: Economist, p. 59, available at the following link: https://asue.am/upload/files/Gitajoxovi-nyuter.pdf
78. "RA GOVERNMENT DEBT MANAGEMENT STRATEGIC PLAN FOR 2022-2024" p. 3, available at the following link:
https://minfin.am/hy/page/partqi_razmavarutyun/
79. RA Ministry of Finance, (2029). "Analysis of the Sustainability of the Government Debt of the Republic of Armenia", p. 19
80. RA Ministry of Finance, (2022). “The Minister of Finance presented the draft state budget of the Republic of Armenia for 2022 in the National Assembly”, available at the following link:
https://minfin.am/hy/content/finansneri_nakhararn_azh-um_nerkayacrel_e_hh_2022t_petakan_byujei_nakhagitsy/#sthash.RmjnyEWx.dpbs
81. MATEVOSYAN, A., & GRIGORYAN, A. (2023). “NEW SOLUTIONS OF PUBLIC DEBT MANAGEMENT IN THE CONTEXT OF DEBT INSTRUMENT SELECTION”. «I Международное книжное издание стран Содружество Независимых Государств / «ЛУЧШИЙ НАУЧНЫЙ СОТРУДНИК - 2023»: I международная книжная коллекция научно-педагогических работников – ISBN 978-601-341-358-7, Астана, 2023 г., с. 38-42

82. Ministry of Finance of the Republic of Armenia, (2021). "TAXO-BUDGETARY POLICY OF THE RA FOR 2022-2024", p. 17, available at the following link:
https://minfin.am/website/images/files/%20%20%202022-2024.docx
83. Matevosyan, A., Grigoryan, A. (2021). “Assessment of the analysis of the sustainability of the RA public debt according to the MAC DSA methodology of the International Monetary Fund”, *"ADVANCE RESEARCH JOURNAL OF MULTIDISCIPLINARY DISCOVERIES" I Vol.68 I Issue-1 I Chapter-1 E-ISSN: 2456-1045,* available at the following link:
http://www.journalresearchijf.com/wp-content/uploads/FM-V68-I1-C1-DEC-2021-PP-01-09.pdf?fbclid=IwAR3RyDu0ls8P9TrJDN4X6-mvWTOd812twXYK_P4uj-RkP9O7zEGI9mjKKYU
84. "The RA Government's Strategic Debt Management Program for 2021-2023", p. 12, available at the following link:
https://minfin.am/hy/page/partqi_razmavarutyun/
85. Hegyan, S., (2023). "13% economic growth recorded in the second quarter, mainly provided by trade and services", available at the following link: https://hetq.am/hy/article/147571 last accessed on 10/01/2023.
86. Petrosyan, G., (2018). "External Shocks and Problems of Ensuring Macroeconomic Stability in the Republic of Armenia", Dissertation No. Г.00.02 for the degree of Candidate of Economics in the specialty "Economics and Management of the Economy, Its Sectors", pp 122-123
87. CBA "Inflation Report/1", (2021). "Monetary Policy Program Implementation Report for the 4th Quarter of 2021", pp. 36-38, available at the following link:
https://www.cba.am/Storage/AM/downloads/parberakan/DVQ/Monetary%20overview_I_2022.pdf
88. "Medium-Term State Expenditure Program of the Republic of Armenia for 2022-2024", pp. 22-24, available at the following link:
https://minfin.am/hy/page/petakan_mijnazhamket_tsakhseri_tsragre/
89. "Revised Program for Reducing the Debt Burden of the RA Government for 2022-2026", p. 4, available at the following link: https://www.e-gov.am/u_files/file/decrees/kar/GV73-6817-ACFF-CBF2/1010.2.pdf
90. GRIGORYAN, A. (2021). "PROBLEMS OF DEBT SECURITY OF THE RA ECONOMY IN THE CONTEXT OF THE ARTSAKH WAR", SCIENTIFIC ARTSAKH № 1(8), 2021, DOI: 10.52063/25792652-2021.1-181 pp. 181-187, available at the following link:
https://arar.sci.am/dlibra/publication/293297/edition/269281

91. "Law of the Republic of Armenia on State Debt", Article 5, available at the following link:
https://www.arlis.am/documentview.aspx?docid=119085
92. "Armenia's public debt is serviced without obstacles during the war", available at the following link:
93. https://minfin.am/hy/content/hayastani_petakan_partqy_paterazmi_orerin_spasarkvum_e_aranc_khochyndotneri/
94. “Revised programs for 2023-2025 state medium-term expenditures and 2022-2026 reduction of the RA government debt burden”, p. 7, available at the following link:
https://minfin.am/hy/page/petakan_mijnazhamket_tsakhseri_tsragre
95. Melkumyan, M. (2015). "Problems of Economic Development of the Republic of Armenia within the Framework of the EAEU"; Proceedings of the 25th ASUE Conference "KNOWLEDGE, INNOVATION AND DEVELOPMENT", Yerevan: Economist, p. 251, available at the following link: https://asue.am/upload/files/II_Baj._tarmacvac.pdf
96. Eurasian Economic Commission Forecast prepared in April-May 2019. Forecast data cutoff date is 15 April 2019. EAEU Member States Main Economic Indicators 2019-2021 Forecast pp. 5-13, available at the following link:
97. http://www.eurasiancommission.org/en/act/integr_i_makroec/dep_makroec_pol/economyPrognoz/Documents/EAEU%20Member%20States%20Forecast_fin.pdf
98. IMF (2020). “World Economic Outlook Database”, available at the following link:
https://www.imf.org/en/Publications/SPROLLs/world-economic-outlook-databases#sort=%40imfdate%20descending
99. World Bank Group (2023). “Global Economic Prospects”, available at the following link:
https://openknowledge.worldbank.org/bitstream/handle/10986/38030/GEP-January-2023.pdf?fbclid=IwAR3Vfu4dbas5MvoHn_dWlvB0dKwds3OeNHXWEIs44IL_EuMs8UztbnX9h08
100. Dynamics of summary data on the debt of the RA government for 2013-2022, available at the following link:
https://www.minfin.am/hy/page/petakan_partqi_veraberyal_ampop_tvyalner/
101. Matevosyan, A., Grigoryan, A., (2023). "THE APPROACH TO ASSESSING THE IMPACT OF ECONOMIC ACTIVITY GROWTH AND FOREIGN EXCHANGE DEBT OF THE RA" INTERNATIONAL SCIENTIFIC

AND EDUCATIONAL CENTER OF THE RA "PROBLEMS OF COMPETITIVE EDUCATION AND SCIENCE IN A RAPIDLY CHANGING WORLD" PROCEEDINGS OF THE INTERNATIONAL SCIENTIFIC CONFERENCE JUNE 21, 2023, ISSN 2579-2903, pp. 327-347,
https://www.isec.am/images/gitakan_hraparakumner/Gitajoxov_2023.pdf
102. GRIGORYAN, A. (2021). "PROBLEMS OF DEBT SECURITY OF THE RA ECONOMY IN THE CONTEXT OF THE ARTSAKH WAR", SCIENTIFIC ARTSAKH № 1(8), 2021, DOI: 10.52063/25792652-2021.1-181 p. 187, available at the following link:
https://arar.sci.am/dlibra/publication/293297/edition/269281
103. Matevosyan, A., Grigoryan, A. (2023). "APPROACHES TO ASSESSING THE INTERACTION BETWEEN RA FOREIGN STATE DEBT AND MACROECONOMIC INDICATORS", "European University" Collection of Scientific Articles 14 (01), 2023, pp. 11-26
104. Ghasemi, A.; Zahediasl, S. (2012). "Normality Tests for Statistical Analysis: A Guide for Non-Statisticians"; 2012. *Int J Endocrinol Metab. 10(2): 486-9. DOI: 10.5812/ijem.3505,* available at the following link:
https://www.ncbi.nlm.nih.gov/pmc/articles/PMC3693611/
105. Field, A. (2009). *Discovering statistics using SPSS.* 3 ed. London: SAGE publications Ltd. p. 822.
106. Driscoll, P.; Lecky, F.; Crosby, M. (2000). An introduction to everyday statistics-1. *J Accid Emerg Med.* 17(3):205–11
107. Pallant, J. (2007). *SPSS survival manual, a step by step guide to data analysis using SPSS for windows.* 3 ed. Sydney: McGraw Hill; 2007. pp. 179–200
108. Royston, P. (1991). "Estimating departure from normality". *Stat Med*;10(8):1283–93.
109. Altman, D.G.; Bland, J.M. (1995). "Statistics notes: the normal distribution". *Bmj*;310(6975):298.
110. Oztuna, D.; Elhan, A.H.; Tuccar, E. (2006). "Investigation of four different normality tests in terms of type 1 error rate and power under different distributions". *Turkish Journal of Medical Sciences*;36(3):171–6
111. Peat, J.; Barton, B. (2005). "*Medical Statistics: A guide to data analysis and critical appraisal*". Blackwell Publishing
112. Thode, H. J. (2002). "*Testing for normality*". New York: Marcel Dekker
113. Elliott, A.C; Woodward, W. A. (2007). "*Statistical analysis quick reference guidebook with SPSS examples*". 1st ed. London: Sage Publications
114. Steinskog, D. J. (2007). 'A cautionary note on the use of the Kolmogorov-Smirnov test for normality". *American Meteor Soc.*135:1151–7

115. Lintner, J. (1965). "Security Prices, Risk, and Maximal Gains from Diversification". The Journal of Finance 20 (4): 587–615.
116. Bunda, Irina, A. Javier Hamann, and Subir Lall. (2009). "Correlations in Emerging Market Bonds: The Role of Local and Global Factors". *Emerging Market Review 10 (2): 67–96.*
117. McGuire, Patrick, and Martijn A. Schrijvers. (2006). "Common Factors in Euro-Denominated Emerging Market Bond Spreads.". *International Finance Review 6: 261–80.*
118. Fidora, Michael, Marcel Fratzscher, and Christian Thimann. (2007). "Home Bias in Global Bond and Equity Markets: The Role of Real Exchange Rate Volatility". *Journal of International Money and Finance 26: 631–55.*
119. Kim, ByoungJoon, Young Sup Yun, BeomCheolCin, and Young Jun Kim. (2014). "Home Bias in Emerging Bond and Stock Markets.". *Emerging Markets Finance and Trade 50 (4): 95–124.*
120. Horioka, Charles, Akiko Terada–Hagiwara, and Takaaki Nomoto (2016). "Explaining Foreign Holdings of Asia's Debt Securities: The Feldstein–Horioka Paradox Revisited."; *Asian Economic Journal 30 (1): 3–24.*
121. Burger, John D., and Francis E. Warnock. (2007). "Foreign Participation in Local Currency Bond Markets". *Review of Financial Economics 16: 291–304.*
122. Aghabekyan, E., (2018). "Are RA Government Bond Yields Overestimated? What to Expect from the Risks Accumulated in the Market?", available at the following link:
https://asue.am/amberd/publications/analytics/profitability-government-bonds-ra-overestimated
123. Feldstein, M., and Horioka, Ch. (1980). "Domestic Saving and International Capital Flows."; *The Economic Journal 90: 314–29.*
124. Chan, Kalok, Vicentiu Covrig, and Lilian Ng. (2005). "What Determines the Domestic Bias and Foreign Bias? Evidence from Mutual Fund Equity Allocations Worldwide"; *The Journal of Finance 60 (3): 1495–534.*
125. Warnock, Francis E., and Veronica C. Warnock. (2009). "International Capital Flows and U.S. Interest Rates". *Journal of International Money and Finance 28 (6): 903–19.*
126. Ferreira, Miguel, and Antonio F. Miguel. (2011). "The Determinants of Domestic and Foreign Bond Bias". *Journal of Multinational Financial Management 21: 279–300.*
127. Pradkhan, E. (2016a). "Impact of Culture and Patriotism on Home Bias in Bond Portfolios."; *Review of Managerial Science 10 (2): 265–301.*

128. Pradkhan, E. (2016b). “Impact of Domestic Investor Protection on Foreign Investment Decisions: Evidence from Bond Markets”. *International Journal of Finance and Economics 21 (4): 417–46.*
129. Eichler, Stefan, and Timo Plaga, (2017). “The Political Determinants of Government Bond Holdings.”; *Journal of International Money and Finance 73 (Part A): 1–21.*
130. Donghyun Park, Kiyoshi Taniguchi, and Shu Tian. (2014). “Foreign and Domestic Investment in Global Bond Markets”. *ADB economics working paper series, NO. 535,* available at the following link:
https://www.adb.org/sites/default/files/publication/396581/ewp-535-foreign-domestic-investment-bond-markets.pdf
131. Fitch ratings (2022). “Fitch Affirms Armenia at 'B+'; Outlook Stable”, available at the following link:
https://www.fitchratings.com/research/sovereigns/fitch-affirms-armenia-at-b-outlook-stable-18-03-2022
132. Fitch Ratings (2023). “Fitch Ratings has revised the Outlook on Armenia's Long-Term Foreign-Currency Issuer Default Rating (IDR) to Positive from Stable and affirmed the IDR at 'B+'” available at the following link:
https://www.fitchratings.com/research/sovereigns/fitch-revises-armenia-outlook-to-positive-affirms-at-b-10-02-2023
133. Grigoryan, A. (2022). "Manifestations of the Behavior and Exchange Rate Impact of Government Bonds Circulating in the RA Capital Market in the Context of External Public Debt Management", pp. 141-145 ("Region and World" 2022, No. 1) periodical, available at the following link: http://geopolitika.am/dir/wp-content/blogs.dir/1/files/2022_1_141_145.pdf
134. Matevosyan, A.; Grigoryan, A. (2022). “Assessment of the analysis of the sustainability of the RA public debt according to the MAC DSA methodology of the International Monetary Fund”; *"ADVANCE RESEARCH JOURNAL OF MULTIDISCIPLINARY DISCOVERIES" I Vol.68 I Issue-1 I Chapter-1 E-ISSN: 2456-1045,* available at the following link:
http://www.journalresearchijf.com/wp-content/uploads/FM-V68-I1-C1-DEC-2021-PP-01-09.pdf?fbclid=IwAR3RyDu0ls8P9TrJDN4X6-mvWTOd812twXYK_P4uj-RkP9O7zEGI9mjKKYU
135. Greenidge, K; Craigwell, R; Chrystol, T.; Drakes, L. (2012). “Threshold Effects of Sovereign Debt: Evidence from the Carribean”, *IMF Working Paper. 157, Washington DC.*

136. Mencinger, J.; Aristovnik, A.; Miroslav, V. (2014). "The Impact of Growing Public Debt on Economic Growth in the European Union". *Amfiteatru Economic Journal* 16(35):403-414.
137. Faye, I; Thiam, D. (2015). "Impacts de l'endettement public sur l'économie sénégalaise", *Direction de la Prévision et des Etudes Economiques (DPEE).*
138. Wade, A. (2015). "Policy-Mix et Croissance Economique dans la Zone UEMOA". *Économies et finances, Université d'Auvergne – Clermont Ferrand I.*
139. Omotosho, B.; Bawa, S.; Doguwa, S. (2016). "Determining the Optimal Public Debt Threshold for Nigeria". *CBN Journal of Applied Statistics* 7(2):1-25
140. Adeniyi, O.; Adekunle, W.; Orekoya, S. "Non-linear Relation between External Debt and Economic Growth in Nigeria: Does the Investment Channel Matter?" Available at the following link:
https://mpra.ub.unimuenchen.de/99975/*MPRA Paper No. 99975*
141. Mary, F.M.; Sunday, K.E.; Haruna, A.T. (2019). "Optimal Government Debt and Economic Performance in Nigeria". *International Journal of Academic Research in Economics and Management Sciences* 8(3):385-399.
142. Ehikioya, B.I; Omankhanlen, A.E.; Osuma, G.O.; Inua, O.I. (2020). "Dynamic Relations Between Public External Debt and Economic Growth in African Countries: A Curse or Blessing?". *Journal of Open Innovation: Technology, Market, and Complexity* 6(3):88.
143. Aziz, D.A; N'Zué, F.F. (2020). "The Ivorian External Debt: Is There a Threshold?". *Journal of Economics and Finance 12(1):01-09.*
144. Greenidge, K.; Craigwell, R.; Chrystol, T.; Drakes, L. (2012). "Threshold Effects of Sovereign Debt: Evidence from the Carribean". *IMF Working Paper. 157, Washington DC.*
145. Mencinger, J.; Aristovnik, A.; Miroslav, V. (2014). "The Impact of Growing Public Debt on Economic Growth in the European Union". *Amfiteatru Economic Journal* 16(35):403-414.
146. Abdoul Aziz Diallo and Felix Fofana N'Zué. (2021). "An econometric analysis: Is there an optimal external debt threshold for Guinea?". *Journal of Economics and International Finance, Vol. 13(3),* pp. 136-142, July-September 2021 DOI: 10.5897/JEIF2021.1140 Article Number: 540E85567961, pp. 139-140, available at the following link:
https://academicjournals.org/journal/JEIF/article-full-text-pdf/540E85567961
147. Kapteyn, A.; de Beaufort W.O., (2001). "Reserve Adequacy in Emerging Market Economies", *IMF Working Paper 01/143, September*, p. 7, available at the following link:
https://www.imf.org/external/pubs/ft/wp/2001/wp01143.pdf

148. Williamson, John. (1973). "International Liquidity: A Survey,"; International Liquidity: Are the Supply and Composition Appropriate? p. 59, available at the following link:
https://www.bostonfed.org/-/media/Documents/conference/28/conf28d.pdf
149. Group of Ten. Report of the Study Group on the Creation of Reserve Assets. 1965, (Ossola Report).
150. IMF (2016). "Guidance Note on The Assessment of Reserve Adequacy and Related Considerations", *The IMF staff report, June*, p. 2
151. IMF (2016). "Annual Report on Exchange Arrangements and ExchangeRestrictions 2016", *International Monetary Fund Washington,* p. 7, available at the following link:
https://www.imf.org/en/Publications/Annual-Report-on-Exchange-Arrangements-and-Exchange-Restrictions/Issues/2017/01/25/Annual-Report-on-Exchange-Arrangements-and-Exchange-Restrictions-2016-43741
152. IMF (2015). "Annual Report on Exchange Arrangements and Exchange Restrictions 2015", *International Monetary Fund Washington,* p. 6, available at the following link:
https://www.imf.org/en/Publications/Annual-Report-on-Exchange-Arrangements-and-Exchange-Restrictions/Issues/2017/01/25/Annual-Report-on-Exchange-Arrangements-and-Exchange-Restrictions-2015-42751
153. IMF (2014). "Annual Report on Exchange Arrangements and Exchange Restrictions 2014" *International Monetary Fund Washington,* p. 5, available at the following link:
https://www.imf.org/en/Publications/Annual-Report-on-Exchange-Arrangements-and-Exchange-Restrictions/Issues/2016/12/31/Annual-Report-on-Exchange-Arrangements-and-Exchange-Restrictions-2014-41643
154. Hausmann, R.; Panizza, U.; Stein, E., (2000). "Why Do Countries Float the Way theyFloat?", Inter-American Dvelopment bank, *May, Working Paper 418*, pp. 4-5
155. Barajas, A.; Erickson, A.; Steiner, R., "Fear of Declaring: Do Markets Care What Countries Say About Their Exchange Rate Policies?", *IMF Staff Papers, Vol. 55, No. 3*
156. Vardanyan, K., J., Avagyan, G., A., Petrosyan, G., A., (2018). "Ensuring a Sufficient Level of International Reserves as a Factor Reducing Economic Vulnerability", Region and World, 2018, No. 4, pp. 85-86, available at the following link:
157. http://test.journals.sci.am/index.php/region_and_world/article/view/3479/3018

158. ATOYAN, K., (2015). "INSTITUTIONAL BASIS AND MANAGEMENT FEATURES OF INTERNATIONAL FOREIGN EXCHANGE RESERVES AT THE CURRENT STAGE", BANBER 2015.(3), pp. 10-11, available at the following link: https://hal.science/hal-03284408/document
159. Fisher, S., (2001). IMF and World Bank "International Reserves Management Policies," conference proceedings, April 28, 2001.
160. Central Bank of the Republic of Armenia, (2022). "Announcement on the Monetary Policy of the Central Bank of the Republic of Armenia", page 1, available at the following link:
https://www.cba.am/Storage/AM/downloads/karger/Arjutaynhaitarar.pdf
161. Source: www.tradingeconomics.com
162. "RA GOVERNMENT DEBT MANAGEMENT STRATEGIC PLAN FOR 2023-2025", p. 13, available at the following link:
https://www.minfin.am/hy/page/partqi_razmavarutyun/
163. Summary indicators of the Central Bank of the Republic of Armenia https://www.cba.am/am/sitepages/statsdds.aspx
164. "MACROECONOMIC AND FISCAL DEVELOPMENTS OF THE REPUBLIC OF ARMENIA IN THE FIRST QUARTER OF 2021", p. 9, available at the following link:
https://www.minfin.am/website/images/files/_2021_I%20%203.docx
165. "State Debt Report" (2021 annual), p. 17, available at the following link: https://minfin.am/hy/page/tarekan_hashvetvutyunner/
166. MATEVOSYAN, A., & GRIGORYAN, A. (2023). "RA STATE DEBT SERVICING CAPACITY IN COLLAPSE SITUATIONS", Scientific-Educational Center of NAS RA "KATCHAR" SCIENTIFIC PERIODICAL, 2023 (1), Yerevan 2023, pp. 50-62
http://katchar.isec.am/myfiles/files/katchar2023.pdf
167. KRUGMAN, P. (2011). "Financing vs. forgiving a debt overhang," *Journal of Development Economics*, 29(3), 253–268: "Self-defeating Austerity," New York Times, July 7
168. DELONG, B. J. AND SUMMERS, L. H. (2012). "Fiscal Policy in a Depressed Economy" . *Brookings Papers on Economic Activity, Spring*
169. COCHRANE, J. H. (2011a, b). "Inflation and Debt," 2011a, *National Affairs, (9), 56–78. (2011b): "Understanding policy in the great recession: Some unpleasant fiscal arithmetic," European Economic Review*, 55(1), 2–30.
170. Panizza, U., Presbitero A. F. (2013). "Public debt and economic growth in advanced economies: A survey". *Working paper 78, Money and Finance Research group (Mo.Fi.R.) - Univ. Politecnica Marche - Dept. Economic and*

Social Sciences, p. 17, available at the following link: https://econpapers.repec.org/paper/ancwmofir/78.htm

171. Slav'yuk, R. & Slaviuk, N. (2018). "Government debt management: challenges and perspectives.". *Investment Management and Financial Innovations,* 15(3), 143-156. doi:10.21511/imfi.15 (3).2018.12

172. Modigliani, F. (1961). "Long-Run Implications of Alternative Fiscal Policies and the Burden of the National Debt". *The Economic Journal*, 71, 730-755. https://doi.org/10.2307/2228247

173. Solberg, R.L. (1988). *"Sovereign Rescheduling: Risk and Portfolio Management". Routledge.*

174. Moreno-Badia; Marialuz; Paulo Medas; Pranav Gupta and Yuan Xiang. (2020). "Debt is Not Free," *IMF Working Paper 20/1 (Washington: International Monetary Fund).*

175. Kumar, M., & Woo, J. (2010). "Public Debt and Growth". *Washington DC: International Monetary Fund, Working Paper*, *WP/10/174*, available at the following link: https://doi.org/10.5089/9781455201853.001

176. João Tovar Jalles and Paulo Medas. (2022). "Economic Growth After Debt Surges". *International Monetary Fund WP/22/159*p. 4, available at the following link:
https://www.imf.org/en/Publications/WP/Issues/2022/07/29/Economic-Growth-After-Debt-Surges-521357

177. Reinhart, C.M.; Rogoff, K.S. (2010). "Growth in a time of debt. 100(2):573–578, available at the following link:
https://www.aeaweb.org/articles?id=10.1257/aer.100.2.573

178. Baum, A.; Checherita-Westphal, C.; and Rother P. (2013). "Debt and Growth: New Evidence for the Euro Area". *Journal of International Money and Finance* 32: 809–21

179. CHECHERITA-WESTPHAL, C. ROTHER, P. (2012). "The Impact of High Government Debt on Economic Growth and Its Channels: An Empirical Investigation for the Euro Area". *European Economic Review, 56, No. 7*, pp. 1392 – 1405.

180. Hadhek Zouhaier, Mrad Fatma. (2014). "Debt and Economic Growth". *International Journal of Economics and Financial Issues Vol. 4, No. 2, pp.440-448 ISSN: 2146-4138p.9,* available at the following link: https://dergipark.org.tr/en/download/article-file/362874

181. Wani, Nassir Ul Haq and Kabir, Habib. (2016). "An evaluation of relationship between public debt and economic growth: A study of Afghanistan"

MPRA Munich Personal RePEc Archive. 19 October, available at the following link:
https://mpra.ub.uni-muenchen.de/75538/1/MPRA_paper_75538.pdf

182. IMF (2008). "External Debt Statistics: Guide for Compilers and Users: External Debt Sustainability Analysis", p. 2, available at the following link: http://tffs.org/pdf/edsg/edsgcha14.pdf

183. Silaeva, A., Doronkina, I., Boboshko, (2020). "Macroeconomic Policy as A Condition for The Formation of Corporate Financial Policy". *N. / Vol. 9 Núm.* 25: 182 -189, available at the following link:

184. https://amazoniainvestiga.info/index.php/amazonia/article/view/1119/1019

185. Moore, W., & Skeete, K. (2010). "The implications of monetary policy shocks for government debt management in Barbados", *CBB Working Paper*

186. Alzyadat, J. (2021). "Public Debt Management and Macroeconomics Policies Coordination". *Evidence from Jordan. Amazonia Investiga, 9(36)*, 59-7, pp. 2-3, available at the following link:
https://doi.org/10.34069/AI/2020.36.12.5

187. Rodrik, D., &Rodriguez, F. (2010). "Trade Policy and Economic Growth: A Skeptic's Guide to the Cross-National Evidence".

188. Bashir Al Hemzawi & Natacha Umutoni. (2021). "Impact of exports and imports on the economic growth: A case study of Rwanda from 2006 to 2020", p. 9, available at the following link:
http://hj.diva-portal.org/smash/get/diva2:1560984/FULLTEXT01.pdf

189. IMF (2003). "External Debt Statistics: Guide for Compilers and Users".*Part III: Use of External Debt Statistics - Debt Sustainability: Medium-Term Scenarios and Debt Ratios*, p. 4, available at the following link: https://www.imf.org/external/pubs/ft/eds/eng/guide/file4.pdf

190. MATEVOSYAN, A., & GRIGORYAN, A. (2023). "PROPOSED BOARD OF PUBLIC DEBT BURDEN ASSESSMENT", Alternative scientific journal, ISSN 1829-2828, 2023 (1), pp. 95-100

191. The European Stability Mechanism (ESM)
https://www.esm.europa.eu/useful-links

192. Central Bank of Armenia: "Standard Table of International Reserves and Foreign Exchange Liquidity 2011-2022 (by months)", available at the following link: https://www.cba.am/am/sitepages/statsdds.aspx

ANNEX 1

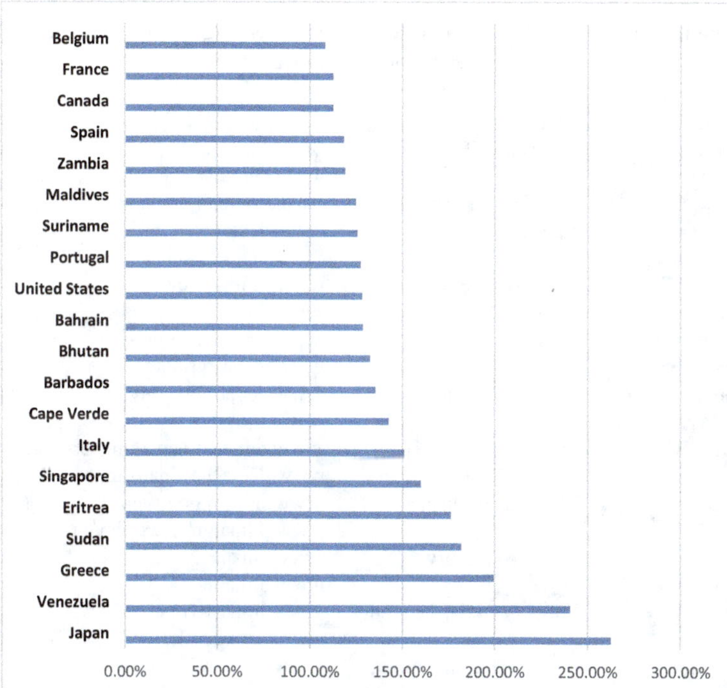

Figure 1. Countries with the highest public debt relative to gross domestic product in 2021[233]

Source www.statista.com

ANNEX 2

Table 1: Ministries of Finance and Debt Management Agencies/Treasuries (if the institution is separate)[234]

Country	Institution	Websites
Austria	Ministry of Finance	www.bmf.gv.at www.oebfa.at
Belgium	Austrian Federal Finance Agency	finances.belgium.be/fr/ www.debtagency.be
Cyprus	Federal Public Service Ministry of Finance	www.centralbank.gov.cy/ www.mof.gov.cy/
Estonia	Belgian Debt Agency	www.fin.ee/
Finland	Central Bank of Cyprus	www.vm.fi/en/frontpage www.treasuryfinland.fi/
France	Ministry of Finance	www.economie.gouv.fr/ www.aft.gouv.fr/
Germany	Ministry of Finance	www.bundesfinanzministerium.de/ www.deutsche-finanzagentur.de/
Greece	Ministry of Finance	www.minfin.gr/?q=en// www.pdma.gr/index.php/en/
Ireland	Finnish Treasury	www.finance.gov.ie/ www.ntma.ie/
Latvia	Ministry of the Economy	www.fm.gov.lv/lv/ www.kase.gov.lv/
Luxembourg	French Treasury Agency	www.mf.public.lu/ www.te.public.lu/
Malta	Ministry of Finance	mfin.gov.mt/en/ www.treasury.gov.mt/
Netherlands	German Debt Management Office	www.rijksoverheid.nl/ www.dsta.nl/
Portugal	Ministry of Finance	www.portugal.gov.pt/en/ministries/mf/the-team.aspx www.igcp.pt/
Slovakia	Public Debt Management Agency	www.finance.gov.sk/ www.ardal.sk/
Slovenia	Finance Department	www.mf.gov.si/
Spain	National Treasury Management Agency Ministry of Finance	www.mineco.gob.es/ www.tesoro.es/

[234] Source: The European Stability Mechanism (ESM) https://www.esm.europa.eu/useful-links

ANNEX 3

Table 1. Verification of the results of the correlation assessment of the indicators of economic activity and external debt of the Republic of Armenia

Parameter	Value
P-value	0.7023
W	0.9675
Sample size (N)	20
Average ($\bar{x}$)	105.135
Median	104.6
Sample Standard Deviation (S)	5.9258
Sum of Squares	667.1855
B	25.4072
Skewness	-0.1553
Skewness Shape	Potentially Symmetrical (pval=0.762)
Excess kurtosis	-0.1131
Kurtosis Shape	Potentially Mesokurtic, normal like tails (pval=0.909)

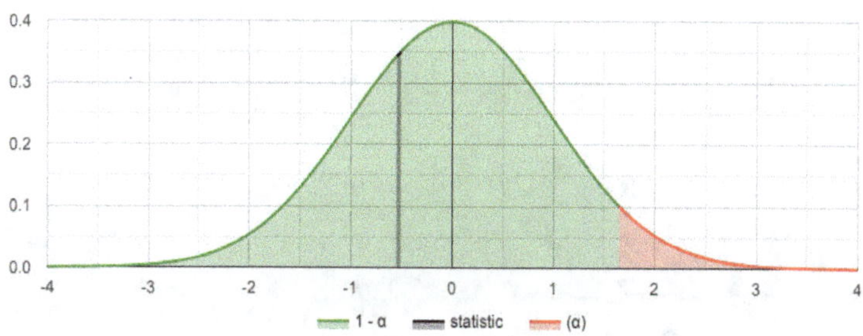

Graph 1. Normal distribution (mean:0, std:1)

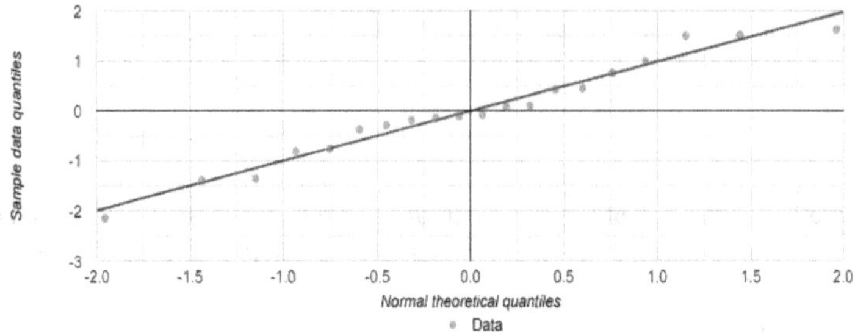

Figure 1. Normal distribution

ANNEX 4

Table 1. Verification of the results of the correlation coefficient estimation of the dollar exchange rate and external debt indicators in the Republic of Armenia

Parameter	Value
P-value	0.09001
W	0.9675
Sample size (N)	20
Average ($\bar{x}$)	105.135
Median	104.6
Sample Standard Deviation (S)	5.9258
Sum of Squares	667.1855
B	25.4072
Skewness	-0.1553
Skewness Shape	Potentially Symmetrical (pval=0.762)
Excess kurtosis	-0.1131
Kurtosis Shape	Potentially Mesokurtic, normal like tails (pval=0.909)

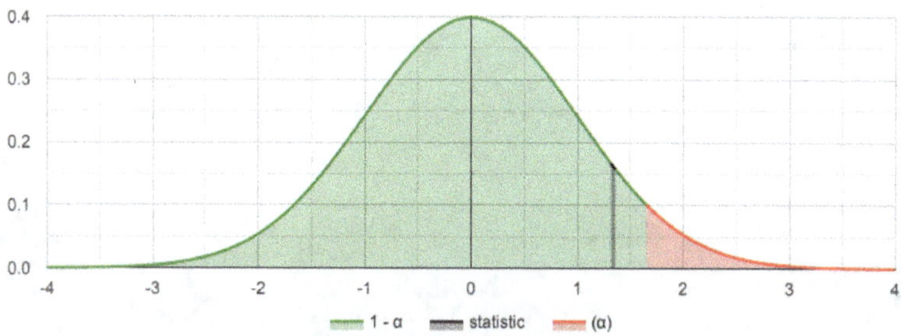

Graph 1. Normal distribution (mean:0, std:1)

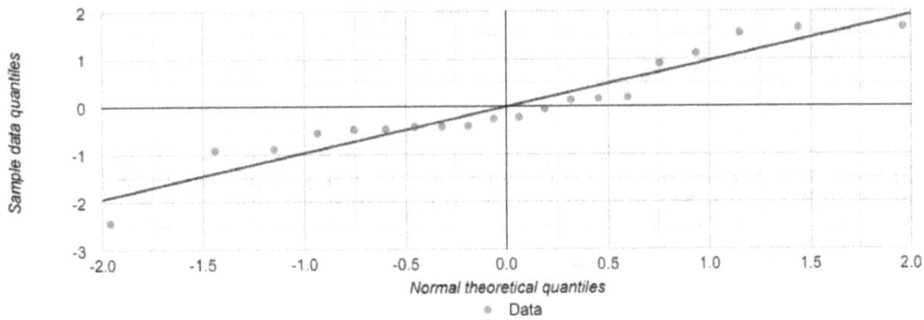

Figure 1. Normal distribution

ANNEX 5

Table 1. Verification of the results of the correlation assessment of the average monthly salary and the volume of bonds placed in the Republic of Armenia

Parameter	Value
P-value	0.0001832
W	0.7622
Sample size (N)	21
Average ($\bar{x}$)	61.0703
Median	92.5
Sample Standard Deviation (S)	65.8925
Sum of Squares	86836.5507
B	257.2692
Skewness	0.7624
Skewness Shape	Potentially Symmetrical (pval =0.128)
Excess kurtosis	0.4778
Kurtosis Shape	Potentially Mesokurtic, normal like tails (pval= 0.623)

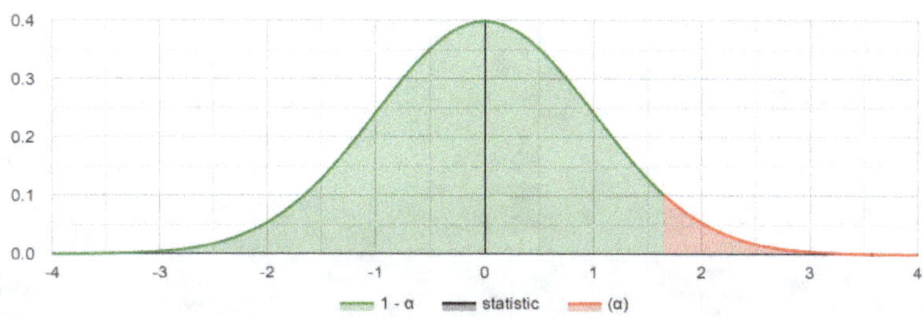

Graph 1. Non-significant correlation

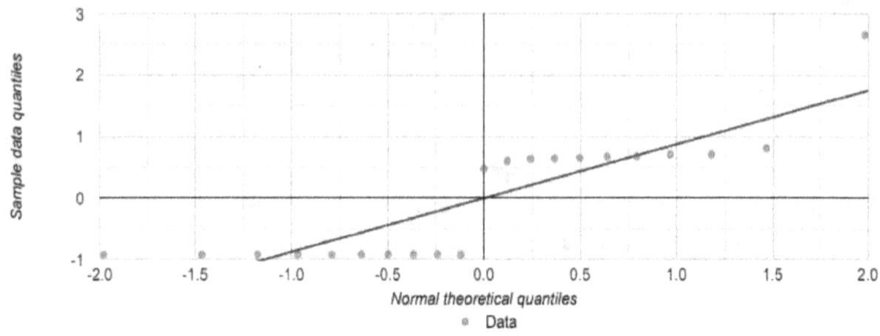

Figure 1. Non-significant correlation

APPENDIX 6

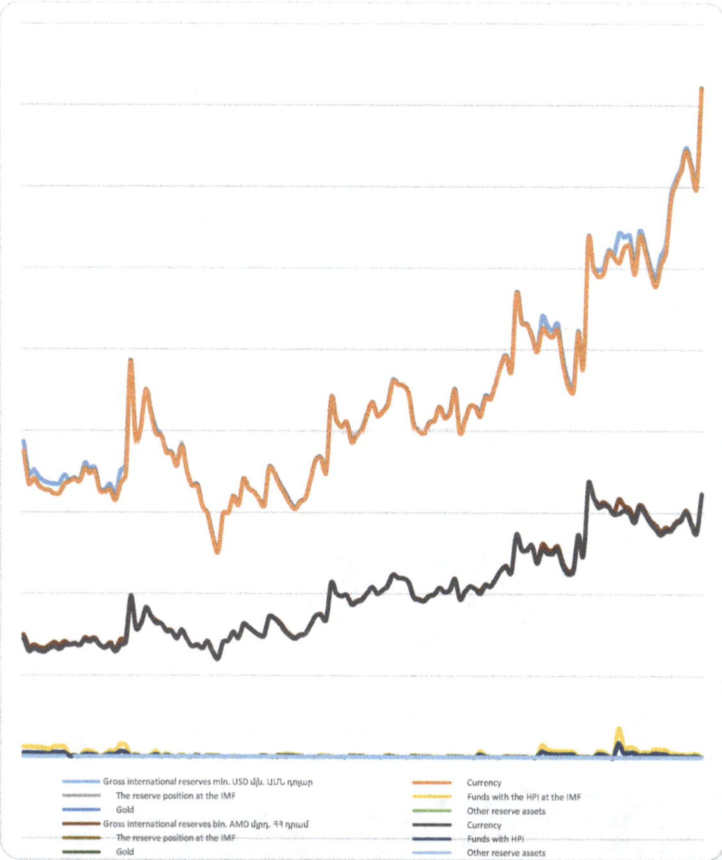

Figure 1. Armenia's international reserves, 2011-2022 (by months)[235]

[235] Central Bank of Armenia: "Standard Table of International Reserves and Foreign Exchange Liquidity 2011-2022 (by months)", available at the following link: https://www.cba.am/am/sitepages/statsdds.aspx

ACKNOWLEDGMENT

I would like to express my gratitude to one person who made this book more readable that it otherwise might have been – Ashot Varazdat Matevosyan. Professor Matevosyan helped me blast my way through the quite substantial barrier between unwieldy early scribblings and something that resembled a book.

Ashot Matevosyan was also enormously helpful in tightening my manuscript during the throes of final drafting.

Finally, I would like to acknowledge with gratitude the support and love of my fiancée who kept me going and this book would not have been possible without them.

Sincerely,

DR. ANI ZOHRAB GRIGORYAN

www.ingramcontent.com/pod-product-compliance
Lightning Source LLC
LaVergne TN
LVHW022054200926
848481LV00003B/912